# MotionGraphicsWEB

EDITED BY
KATHLEEN ZIEGLER
NICK GRECO
TAMYE RIGGS

WATSON-GUPTILL

an imprint of HarperCollins International

First Published 2002 by:
HBI, an imprint of
HarperCollins Publishers
10 East 53rd Street
New York, NY 10022-5299

Distributed in the US and Canada by:
Watson-Guptill Publications
770 Broadway
New York, NY 10022-5299
Phone: 800.451.1741 or 732.363.4511 in NJ, AK, HI
Fax: 732.363.0338

ISBN 0-8230-3142-X

Distributed throughout the rest of the world by:
HarperCollins International
10 East 53rd Street
New York, NY 10022-5299
Fax: 212.207.7654

ISBN 0-06-008760-9

Address Direct Mail Sales to:
Dimensional Illustrators, Inc.
362 Second Street Pike / # 112
Southampton, Pennsylvania 18966 USA
215.953.1415  Telephone
215.953.1697  Fax
Email: dimension@3dimillus.com

Printed in Hong Kong.

©Copyright 2002 by Dimensional Illustrators, Inc. and HBI, an imprint of HarperCollins Publishers.

CREDITS

Creative Director / Creative Editor
**Kathleen Ziegler  Dimensional Illustrators, Inc.**

Executive Editor
**Nick Greco  Dimensional Illustrators, Inc.**

Contributing Editor
**Tamye Riggs**

Design and Typography
**Deborah Davis  Deborah Davis Design**

Artwork
Page 7, 158 ©2002 **Honest**

Page 8-9 ©2002 **Move Design**

# TABLE OF CONTENTS

Frank Lloyd Wright 46

The Place 54

Simian 64

eMovie Website 74

scrEAm taBÚ

scrEAm taBÚ 56

Interactive portfolio Portfolio interactivo 1024x768 min.

TUESDAE

Tuesdae Website 66

Mire 76

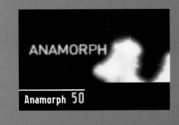
NIGHTMARES

Nightmares 48

M

Move Design Reel 58

American Dream 68

Nebula 78

ANAMORPH

Anamorph 50

INTERACTIVE MEDIA DESIGN REVIEW

WINNERS — ALL

I.D. Magazine 60

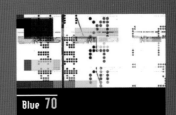
Blue 70

DESC... AVANT!

PWR 80

mY pEt sKeLeTOn 52

IKDA CD-ROM 62

Factory 72

Red 82

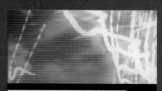
Super Highway of Light 84

Ifilm Pre-Roll 1 94

Yobun No 49 104

Crash Intro 2 114

Baroque 86

Let's Entertain 96

The System 106

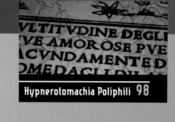
Circus2K1 88

Hypnerotomachia Poliphili 98

Empathy 116

M.O.P. Music Video 90

American Center for Design 100

The Diver 108

Overeactive 118

Ifilm Pre-Roll 2k 92

Formsmart 102

33-1/3k 110

Scan 112

Graffiti Dance 120

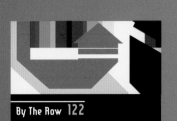

MotionGraphics Web explores the limitless possibilities for creatives working in the new media culture. This eclectic international showcase of digital work features sensory experiences designed to inform, inspire and entertain. Twenty-five stellar design studios present a comprehensive overview of electrifying action visuals created for the web and other interactive media. Seventy-five motion projects from Canada, the Czech Republic, France, Germany, Japan, Spain, Sweden, the United Kingdom and the United States push the boundaries of design, exposing a new creativity to an international audience. Fresh concepts and the latest production techniques, combined with stylish type treatments, dynamic motion effects, provocative visuals and catchy soundtracks, make contemporary

web surfing an unforgettable experience. Websites, Screen Trailers, QuickTime Videos, Interactive Music Flyers, Flash Music Videos, CD-ROMs, Animated Logos, Interactive Documentaries, Demo Reels, Online Video Games, Short Films and Personal Playgrounds are but a few of the innovative works available in the digital arena. Cutting-edge software, high energy and a brave new world of inspiration afford multi-media savvy designers the means to revolutionize the creative communications industry. This exhilarating journey through cyberspace and beyond is a digital dreamscape designed to educate, stimulate and motivate the viewer on the other side of the screen.

—Dimensional Illustrators, Inc.

## Art Director's Club of New York Winner's Website

Platinum Design's goal was to create an entertaining and festive site to showcase the work of the Art Director's Club 80th Awards Show. ADCNY uses the tag line, "PUMPING VISUAL FUEL WORLDWIDE," and the designers took full advantage of the opportunity to play with the theme. This engaging site was built using text and visual elements taken from the world of gas stations, including the use of section buttons designed like rolling prices on old-fashioned gas pumps. Achieving a high level of originality, while providing a fun and well-designed environment for the viewer, is key to the Platinum Design creative philosophy.

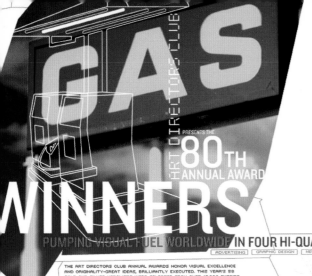
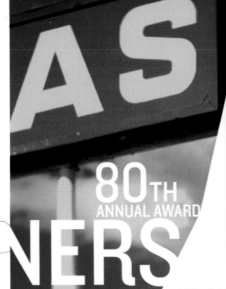

**GAS**

ART DIRECTORS CLUB

PRESENTS THE

**80TH ANNUAL AWARD**

**WINNERS**

PUMPING VISUAL FUEL WORLDWIDE IN FOUR HI-QUALITY GRADES

ADVERTISING | GRAPHIC DESIGN | NEW MEDIA | PHOTO / ILLUS.

THE ART DIRECTORS CLUB ANNUAL AWARDS HONOR VISUAL EXCELLENCE AND ORIGINALITY-GREAT IDEAS, BRILLIANTLY EXECUTED. THIS YEAR'S 58 GOLD AND SILVER MEDALISTS WERE SELECTED FROM OVER 17,000 ENTRIES TO EXEMPLIFY THE TOP WORK OF THE YEAR IN PRINT AND BROADCAST ADVERTISING, MAGAZINE DESIGN, ILLUSTRATION, PHOTOGRAPHY, WEB SITES, INTERFACE, AND CD-ROM DESIGN. THE 80TH ANNUAL EXHIBITION WILL BE ON VIEW AT THE ADC GALLERY IN NEW YORK FROM JUNE 7 THROUGH JULY 31, THEN TRAVELS NATIONALLY AND INTERNATIONALLY THROUGHOUT THE YEAR.

---

ADVERTISING | GRAPHIC DESIGN | NEW MEDIA | PHOTO / ILLUS.

**NEW MEDIA**

**GOLD**

WWW.HTV2.CO.UK
WEBSITE, CD-ROM AND BANNER DESIGN: PRODUCT ADVERTISING, SINGLE

WWW.MOTIONTHEORY.COM
WEBSITE, CD-ROM AND BANNER DESIGN: SELF-PROMOTION, SINGLE

**SILVER**

SCOUT
WEBSITE, CD-ROM AND BANNER DESIGN: PRODUCT ADVERTISING, CAMPAIGN

WWW.FJALLFJLL.COM
WEBSITE, CD-ROM AND BANNER DESIGN: PRODUCT ADVERTISING, CAMPAIGN

NARRATIVE SPACES: WWW.ANNERTAHER.COM
WEBSITE, CD-ROM AND BANNER DESIGN: PRODUCT ADVERTISING, SINGLE

LARAMARA FOUNDATION'S HOTSITE
WWW.THUNDERHOUSE.COM.BR/AWARDS/LARAMARA
WEBSITE, CD-ROM AND BANNER DESIGN: INSTITUTIONAL PROMOTION, SINGLE

WWW.BEIJINGZOO.COM
WEBSITE, CD-ROM AND BANNER DESIGN: SELF-PROMOTION, SINGLE

PLANE MODULATOR
WEBSITE, CD-ROM AND BANNER DESIGN: HYBRID / ART / EXPERIMENTAL, SINGLE

ART DIRECTORS CLUB

80TH ANNUAL AWARD

GARAGE · FUEL

**WINNERS**

PUMPING VISUAL FUEL WORLDWIDE IN FOUR HI-QUALITY GRADES

## Matthew Salacuse Showcase

Manhattan's Platinum Design created Salacuse.com around the concept of building an internet-based apartment/neighborhood to house Matthew Salacuse's photography work. Rather than merely showing beautifully shot photos on a plain background, the designers wanted to create an environment which the audience could literally enter. A simple and effective single-page interface allows visitors to view all photos in the Salacuse online portfolio without incurring additional loading time. The photographer's body of work includes a wide range of subjects, and it seemed amusingly appropriate to mix them in their own digital housing complex. Salacuse is a New York native, and that's what New York is all about; finding the perfect dwelling in a sea of small, tiny, expensive apartments.

12

## Lunchbox Broadcast Design Reel One

Established as an independent type foundry in 1991, Lunchbox has expanded into an agency with print, web, identity and broadcast capabilities. Lunchbox founder Adam Roe wanted a reel that would reflect the studio's diverse body of work, while continuing to emphasize its strong roots in the typographic arts. The design team had the freedom to experiment with new methods of invigorating the screen. The studio's first reel incorporates stylish elements from the Lunchbox web site, and features 3D cityscapes, filmed type played through an 8mm projector and snowboarders flying overhead through parabolic mirrors.

14

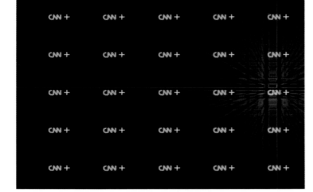

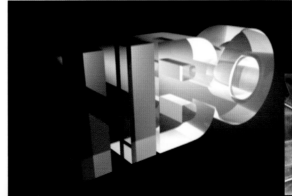

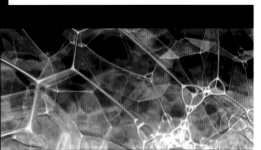

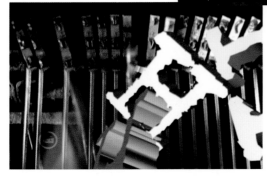

**Control the Chaos**

"Control the Chaos," an evocative website short from Karma Graphix, was designed to express a personal sense of control that gets lost, then is re-acquired. Using strong visual and sound syncopation, the designers combined vector images and type treatments with film sequences to create this moody, sometimes eerie, piece. Using a mixture of different media types, facilitates the crossing over of the conventional styles typically associated with each. The San Francisco based studio's creative style tends to be edgy and open to creative interpretation. Karma Graphix constantly strives for a unique combination of ideas and media to produce pieces that shatter pre-existing conceptual boundaries and challenge established perceptions.

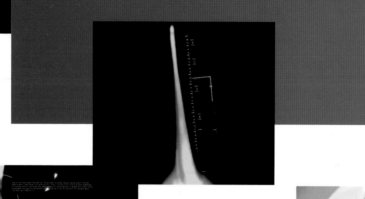

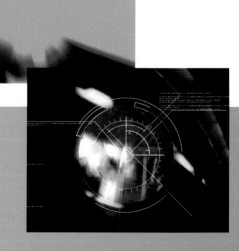

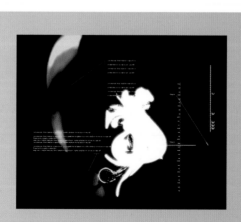

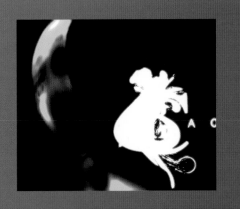

## 3e Oeil Website

French interactive agency Troisième Oeil wanted to create a smart design experience to showcase their body of work. With limited time and budget available for development, 3e oeil.com took inspiration from both the elegance of fine art and the modern elements of a techno environment—software, mobile phones and digital typefaces. Images were shot with a 2-megapixel numeric camera—sequences were mainly two frames per second films. The 3e oeil team uses all available means to enhance the relationship between environments, users and products. Behind each project's unique visual style remains the studio's primary goal—creating attractive, easy to use design.

**18**

# TROISIEME ŒIL
## DESIGN D'INTERACTIONS

**3E ŒIL**

MotionGraphics **Web**

# open

↘

## www.3e-oeil.com

D E F G H I J K L M N O P Q R S T U V W X Y Z a b c d e f g h i  k l m n o

We would be delighted to have your immediate
reactions to our site. Please write to us at feedback@3e-oeil.com

direct access

**Methodology**

Although our concepts and creations are
treated in the most inventive and original
way, our methodology is based upon proven
processes established with design and communication, comprising four stages.

**Definir**
**Dessiner**
**Déve**lopper
**Déployer**

3E ŒIL
- News
- Vision
- Methodology
- Humans

**19**

We would be delighted to have your immediate
reactions to our site. Please write to us at feedback@3e-oeil.com

direct access

**Vision**

The consumer is all too often forgotten or
under estimated in a process where he is the
principal role player. By recognising the
subtle mix of intuition and the sensibilities of
human behaviour and looking at new technologies, we are able to exploit their mutual
relation ship.
The objective today is no longer just to see
design as a form of expression but rather as
a valuable resource which requires regular
re-examination in three areas:

Technology
Form
Function

**V**
**I S**
**I O N**

3E ŒIL
- News
- Vision
- Methodology
- Humans

We would be delighted to have your immediate
reactions to our site. Please write to us at feedback@3e-oeil.com

direct access

...remains, and will continue to do so
...to come, the most popular form of
...on. As complementary to new
...ce is assured and incontestable.
...and graphic composition continues
to develop in both form and support. Constantly
evolving, we are still fascinated by this traditional form of communication mainly because of
its importance in accompanying digital communication - reinforcing the need to maintain open
access between analogue and digital technology. Traditional graphics as we know them con-
stitute the starting blocks for creation of brand
image: logos, design guidelines and packaging
etc.

PROFESSION

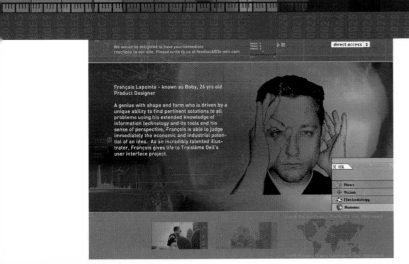

We would be delighted to have your immediate
reactions to our site. Please write to us at feedback@3e-oeil.com

direct access

**François Lapointe - known as Boby, 26 yrs old**
**Product Designer**

A genius with shape and form who is driven by a
unique ability to find pertinent solutions to all
problems using his extended knowledge of
information technology and its tools and his
sense of perspective, François is able to judge
immediately the economic and industrial poten-
tial of an idea. As an incredibly talented illustrator, François gives life to Troisieme Oeil's
user interface project.

3E ŒIL
- News
- Vision
- Methodology
- Humans

## One Thousand Dreams

20

Luis Escorial, a designer with Juxt Interactive, created One Thousand Dreams as a personal expression of his art. From Japanese Kabuki to a magician's performance, motion is a key element in creating mood and tempo, and presenting an experience beyond simple information delivery. It is an experimental ground for motion graphics and narrative—a world of storytellers, where motions become emotions. The site illustrates Escorial's diverse methods of working with motion graphics—from abstract concepts to more linear and cinematographic narratives. One Thousand Dreams is about experience design and the power to engage the audience.

dream n.: 1. a series of thoughts, images or emotions occurring during sleep
2. a visionary creation of the imagination
3. a state of mind marked by abstraction or release from reality

SOUND OFF

One Thousand Dreams

ARE YOU A DREAMER?

SOUND OFF

One Thousand Dreams

### One Thousand Dreams

There is a fiction living between my dreams

WHO WILL TAKE YOUR DREAMS AWAY
TAKES YOUR SOUL ANOTHER DAY

I AM ALWAYS DOING WHAT
I CANNOT DO YET, IN ORDER TO LEARN
HOW TO DO IT.
VINCENT VAN GOGH

../PROJECTS

../01/01  ../01/05
../01/02
../01/03
../01/04

../ ROLL OVER PROJECTS
AND CLICK
TO LAUNCH.

HOME
../01/PROJECTS
../02/CONTACT
../03/DREAMERS        ../1000DREAMS/dreams_v2/spring_01

One Thousand Dreams

ARE YOU A DREAMER?

A WALL OF WORDS

EVEN THOUGH I CAN IMAGINE MYSELF
SAYING TO MY FATHER HOW MUCH I LOVE HIM...

luis ESCORIAL

ms.com

SOUND OFF

WE BOTH USED TO DREAM H

# Billabong

WebsiteBillabong | DesignersTodd Purgason, Paul Nguyen, Josh Forstat ProgrammersBrian Drake, Phil Scott

Juxt Interactive created this website to reinforce the Billabong brand as one of the hottest names in the extreme sports market targeting surf, skate and snow aficionados. The three subsections of the site were designed to express the energy of each sport. Surf was based on the motion of liquid, as a surfer riding a wave. Skate is a juxtaposition of the incredible raw tension of street skate and the fluid dynamics of a grid. Snow, which also carries reflections of snowboarding design, is about the random ride achieved by repeating the same run. The rugged elegance of the sports, entangled with an overall punk aesthetic, is showcased in a rich interactive experience that both informs and entertains.

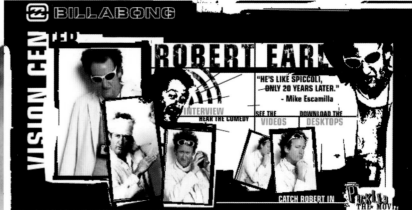

# deCONSTRUCTION

**24**

Designed to promote the sale of the Flash deCONSTRUCTION book, Juxt Interactive wanted to extend the reading experience into an interactive showcase. The deCONSTRUCTION site was based on unveiling pieces of a whole, broken down into digestible chunks. The content is displayed as the user investigates deeper—opening pockets of information not accessible from the surface. Based on the act of reading a book, the viewer must commit to exploring the site to reach the final payoff. Motion and content are revealed by a small arrow moving around the screen, guiding the user's eye and disclosing content and link cues. The cursor acts as a metaphor for the authors, uncovering hidden secrets designed to tantalize the audience.

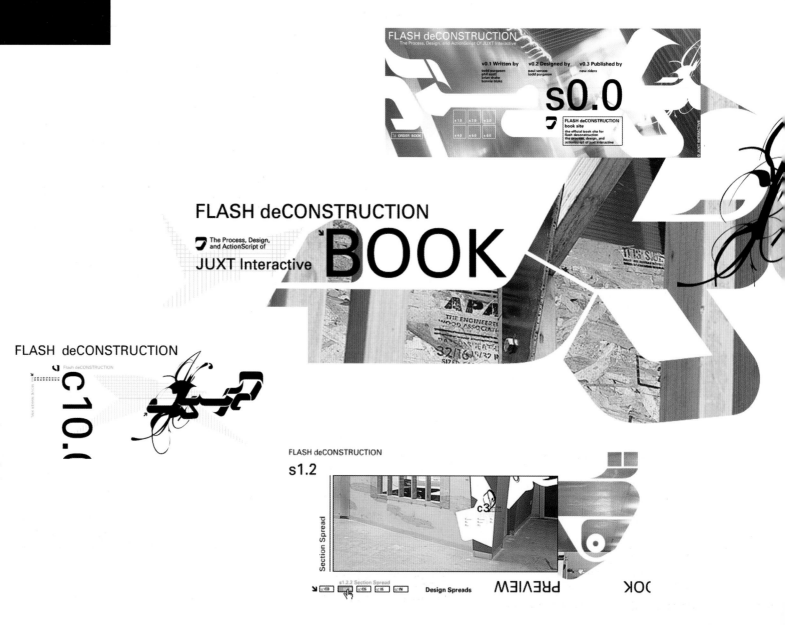

StudioJuxt Interactive

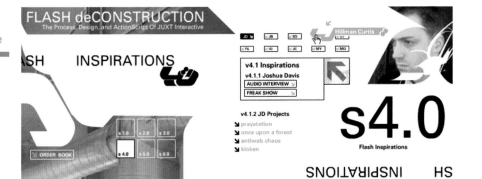

FLASH deCONSTRUCTION
The Process, Design, and ActionScript Of JUXT Interactive

ASH    INSPIRATIONS

Hillman Curtis

v4.1 Inspirations
v4.1.1 Joshua Davis
AUDIO INTERVIEW
FREAK SHOW

v4.1.2 JD Projects
↘ praystation
↘ once upon a forest
↘ antiweb chaos
↘ kioken

ORDER BOOK

s 1.0    s 2.0    s 3.0
s 4.0    s 5.0    s 6.0

s4.0
Flash Inspirations

SH INSPIRATIONS HS

FLASH deCONSTRUCTION

Joshua Davis

s4.1
v4.1.4.1 Polaroid Shoot

SH deCONSTRUCTION
BOOK

ss, Design,
nScript of

Interactive

active.com/deCONSTRUCTION

FLASH deCONSTRUCTION

Mike Young

p07

s4.9
v4.9.4.1 Polaroid Shoot

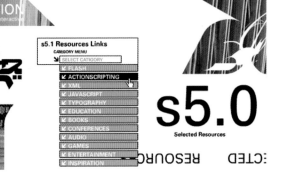

FLASH deCONSTRUCTION
The Process, Design, and ActionScript Of JUXT Interactive

ECTED    RESOURCES

s5.1 Resources Links
CATEGORY MENU
↘ SELECT CATEGORY
↙ FLASH
↙ ACTIONSCRIPTING
↙ XML
↙ JAVASCRIPT
↙ TYPOGRAPHY
↙ EDUCATION
↙ BOOKS
↙ CONFERENCES
↙ AUDIO
↙ GAMES
↙ ENTERTAINMENT
↙ INSPIRATION

ORDER BOOK

s 1.0    s 2.0    s 3.0
s 4.0    s 5.0    s 6.0

s5.0
Selected Resources

CTED RESOURC

## Pickled TV

The Pickled TV site was developed by Juxt Interactive to promote the surf film, "Pickled", a quirky Billabong production. The concept behind the Pickled site is derived from the world of a circus poster gone awry, with a twist of hallucination thrown in the mix for good measure. The site mirrors the tongue-in-cheek nature of the film itself, and is not meant to be taken too seriously. The typography becomes alive through motion, imparting the hallucinatory sense that common inanimate objects have suddenly come to life. The motion trips crazily over itself as if drunk. This tipsy visual style is appropriate, as intoxication plays a major role in the film's plot.

26

CONTEST PICK THE PICKLED VIDEO/DVD ARTWORK & "WIN" (OR MAYBE NOT)

CLICK CLICK CLICK

[ SO TELL ME WHAT I MIGHT WIN DON PARDO! ]

Pick•led

PICKLED [BIGGER]

PICKLED [BIGGER]

PICKLED [BIGGER]

CLICK TO SELECT

NAME
EMAIL
PHONE

[ SEND IT ]

PICKLED THE★MOVIE

NAVIGATION

SITE BY JUXT INTERACTIVE

PiCKLeD
THE★MOVIE

MOVIE MAKER

A FILM BY HIGH VOLTAGE ★ BILLABONG

MIX "YOUR" OWN VERSION ★ THE PiCKLeD MOVIE

[ I WANNA MIX ]

(OK! SO IT'S NOT THE WHOLE MOVIE. JUST PLAY ALONG DAMN IT!)

MOVIE MAKER

PiCKLeD THE★MOVIE

NAVIGATION

SITE BY JUXT INTERACTIVE

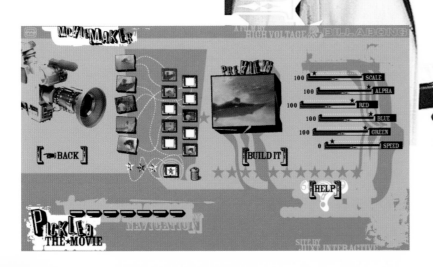

MOVIE MAKER

A FILM BY HIGH VOLTAGE ★ BILLABONG

PREVIEW

100 ★ SCALE
100 ★ ALPHA
100 ★ RED
100 ★ BLUE
100 ★ GREEN
0 ★ SPEED

[ BACK ]

[ BUILD IT ]

[ HELP ]

PiCKLeD THE★MOVIE

NAVIGATION

SITE BY JUXT INTERACTIVE

TURD GAME

A FILM BY HIGH VOLTAGE ★ BILLABONG

SAVE ROBERT EARL ★ & HIS PICKLE FROM RABID SEAGULLS

(OR HELP HIM DIE...DEPENDS ON YOUR PERSPECTIVE)

[ PLAY THE GAME ]

WANNABE OUR HERO IS STRANDED IN THE MIDDLE OF THE PACIFIC WITH ONLY HIS DINGY AND ONE JAR OF PICKLES. WITH OR WITHOUT YOUR HELP HE IS SURE TO KEEL. THE REAL POINT OF THE GAME IS REALLY CHEAP LAUGHS!

PiCKLeD THE★MOVIE

NAVIGATION

SITE BY JUXT INTERACTIVE

## Ericsson Mobile Internet Screen Trailer

Swedish design studio Houdini developed this screen trailer as an extension of Ericsson's global Mobile Internet campaign, which aired during the fall and winter of 2000–01. A calm, harmonic, soundless loop, its primary goal was to get visitors at seminars and conferences to stop and look at a kiosk display. The visual language builds on Ericsson's branding guidelines, with animations designed specifically to fit each photographic image. Single words representing core aspects of the branding message were linked to corresponding photos and given strong visual emphasis. Using eye-catching entertainment tools like Ericsson Mobile Internet Screen Trailer, Houdini creates high-impact, interactive communications for all their clients.

mine

The new personalized Internet. It's more than mobile. It's personalized.

proven

Ericsson backbone networks. Tried, tested and ready.

Ericsson mobile infotainment. What you want. Where you want it.

want

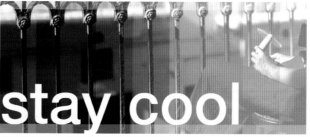

stay cool

Mobile security from Ericsson. Worry free mobile transactions.

Photographer**Kelvin Murray**  Agents**Jo Talbot & Sue Young**  Studio**Houdini Digital Creations**

Ericsson one-mailbox messaging. Keeping your life together.

# pick

Mobile Internet services from Ericsson. Right size. Right design.

mooth

Ericsson system solutions. Evolve to 3G, lump-free.

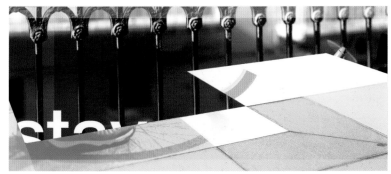

Ericsson backbone networks. Tried, tested and ready.

pick

Mobile Internet services from Ericsson. Right size. Right design.

## Yigal Azrouel Website

Relatively unknown to American audiences, Israeli fashion designer Yigal Azrouel asked New York's Firstborn Multimedia to create an outstanding site that would generate interest in his work. The studio approached the project with great inspiration taken from Azrouel's model photography. Interactive ideas were developed along with graphics, and were organically incorporated into the final design. The distinctive feature of this website is that the user generates dynamic motion effects by interacting with the images on the screen. For their client list of notable fashion, cosmetics and entertainment industry names, Firstborn Multimedia invents memorable experiences on the web.

30

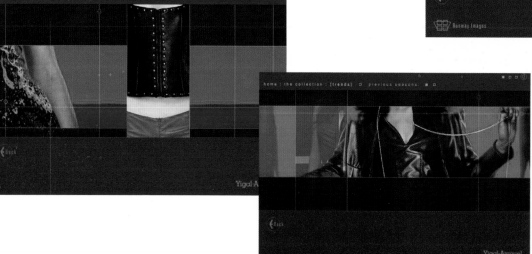

Designer**Sarah McLoughlin** Designer/Flash Programmer**Shea Gonyo** Flash Programmer**Josh Ott**

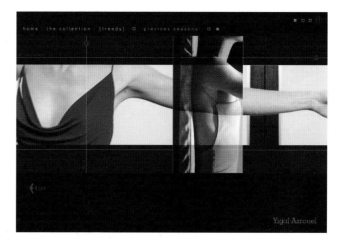

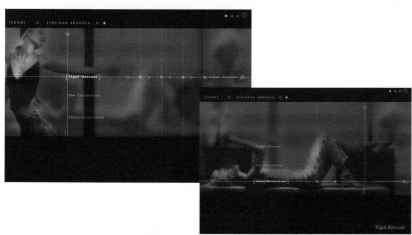

## Uzik Website

"Producing digital content that creates a buzz" is what Uzik is all about. The French design studio continually explores the interaction between sound and imagery to create a "cocktail of the senses." To demonstrate this to an artistically aware audience, they built an elegant and contemporary inter-face to showcase their work. The Uzik portfolio includes a collection of websites, mixers and interactive flyers for musical artists including Bob Sinclar, Madonna, Bjork, AIR and Morcheeba. Uzik Studio spe-cializes in online promotion for the entertainment industry—launching new artists, albums, movies, concert tours and other events for major record labels, entertainment com-panies and ad agencies.

**32**

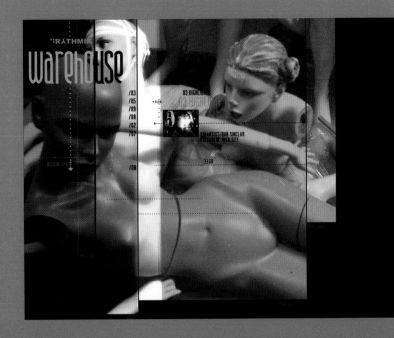

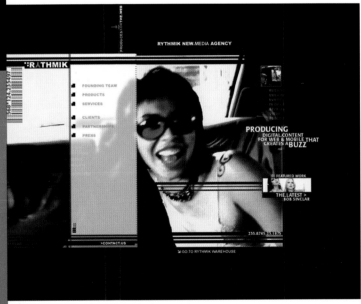

# TORONTO**JUNGLE**.COM

## torontojungle.com Intro

In order to flaunt his home-town's thriving drum and bass scene, Alex Shoukas created a video sequence designed for maximum visual stimulation. With the 2001 winter music conference approaching, toron-tojungle.com was ready for promotion with a CD-ROM designed to tout the well-developed Toronto drum and bass scene to an American audience. Shoukas prepared a QuickTime intro to launch the CD, using torontojungle.com's footage from local events. To achieve his objective, he over-laid footage of bright lights, giving the viewer hints of the underlying footage. The text glows over the footage similar to the way natural light streaks appear. The careful combina-tion of sound, live performance video and digital effects mirrors the excitement of this unique music culture.

**34**

TORONTOJUNGLE.COM

## e.sthetics

Striving for a unique way to say "thank you," Alex Shoukas delivered a powerful message with e.sthetics. After spending two years in Toronto's CyberARTS program, Shoukas discovered his true passion in design. An abbreviation of "electronic aesthetics," e.sthetics was the young designer's final independent study project and homage to his supporters. Controlling the keyframe velocity to maintain fluid motion in the shapes and the text were critical in this piece. Equally important were the careful use of digital photography and some 3-D animation. To avoid a consistent look, he used a variety of shots to hold viewer interest throughout the movie.

36

miss it.

E.STHET

i miss it.

79

miss it.

E.S

thank you ricky

bruised eyes/ derived disquized by cover girl/ dispized by rest of world

E.STHETICS

## SHOWCASE ONTARI

**Showcase Ontario Video Clips**

Exemplifying the speed and innovation of contemporary information technologies, Canadian designer Alex Shoukas created a striking series of video pieces for a sophisticated audience. These video clips were created for the awards presentation ceremonies of Ontario's IT Corporations. Using provided footage as the foundation for each piece, Shoukas then overlaid text and vector outlines of images that related to each awards category. Masking techniques were added to the effects and kept up with the motion of the video. The fast-paced sequences captured the attention of the award show's design and tech-savvy audience.

**38**

QuickTime Video **Showcase Ontario Video Clips** | Designer **Alex Shoukas** Studio **Victoria Graphics**

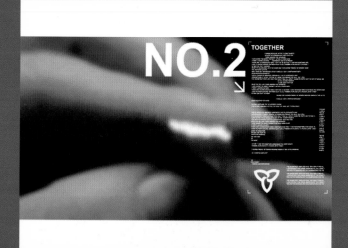

PRIVATE/PUBLIC

PRIVATE/PUBLIC

NERSHIPS

WCASE NTARIO 2000

N TRANSFORMATIO

NOVA

Le.Clash

40

As a designer at French interactive studio UZIK, Frank Borsato has the opportunity to create pioneering work for some of the top names in the music business. When Sony asked him for a new concept in entertainment promotion, the UZIK team created this visually cool interactive sound flyer for NMT Le.Clash. The flyer permits the users to mix their own sound using computer keystrokes, offers a unique level of interaction for its audience, and can be used to promote future musical artists.

IV MY PEOPLE

LE CLASH
BOSS

AGE.35
TAILLE.175CM
POIDS.68KG
TOUR DE COU.39CM
TOUR DE POITRINE.92CM
TOUR DE BICEPS.47CM

LE CLASH
BOSS
IV MY PEOPLE

**NavajoWhite.com**

French designer Frank Borsato built this site as a personal playground and venue to show his diverse portfolio. NavajoWhite.com and its companion subsite, moodspirit.com, feature a selection of his work for musical artists, record labels, movie studios and other entertainment industry clients, as well as his own explorations into online motion design. Incorporating dynamic, almost movie-like animation in his Flash productions, Borsato's work is based on his mood at any given moment, rather than adhering to a rigid design philosophy.

42

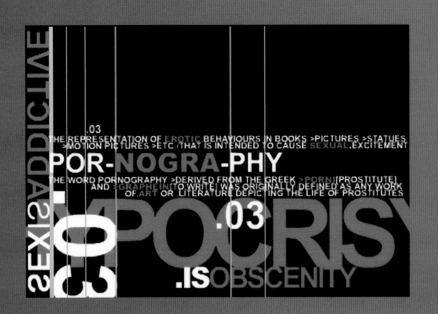

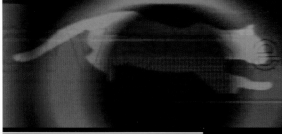

## Discovery Kiosk: Biodiversity

R/GA's challenge was to use technology to translate the Discovery Channel's experiential philosophy into another medium—an interactive game located on a kiosk. The goal was to build a compelling, interactive educational experience that would leverage the brand and appeal to a broad range of users. R/GA designed and created the visually striking biodiversity experience to support the Discovery Channel's core values of exploration, education and adventure. The kiosk, located in the Singapore zoo, provides a place for visitors to learn more about biodiversity and acquire tools for exploring their world.

**David Goldfarb, John Jones** Visual Designers**Lesli Karavil, Vander McClain, Haejin Cho, Winston Thomas, Yzabelle Munson, Jesse McGowan** Programmer**John Jones**

THE GUGGENHEIM
A TEMPLE TO ART

## Frank Lloyd Wright

Interactive Television Broadband Documentary **Frank Lloyd Wright** Studio**R/GA** Creative Director**Peter Stonier**

**46**

R/GA developed this interactive companion piece to Ken Burns' PBS documentary on the celebrated architect Frank Lloyd Wright. Of critical importance was creating a rich learning experience utilizing technology that supported the high-speed delivery of digital information, while maintaining the quality that viewers expect from a Burns production. The resulting piece delivers a level of interactivity that is impossible to achieve in traditional television media and is essentially a virtual tour of the architect's most famous building. The project includes video, text and QuickTime VR tours. An elegant interface allows users to navigate easily through the building, while incorporating the horizontal stratification that characterizes Wright's distinctive work.

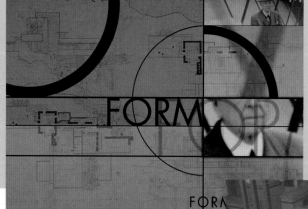

Art Director**Vincent Lacava** Producer**Amy Smith** Designer**Haejin Cho** Programmers**John Jones, Casey Mandell**

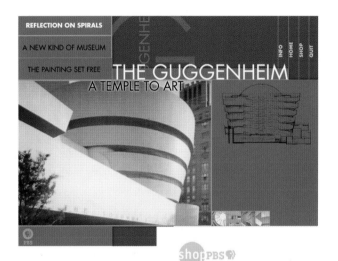

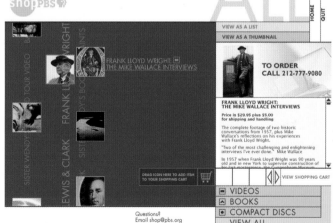

## Nightmares

**48**

Nightmares is an original content site created by New York's WDDG for the DistantCorners.com Original Sins horror channel. DistantCorners.com came to WDDG with the simple premise of creating a content site built around nightmares. In their typically flexible creative style, WDDG created the content-rich and creepy-cool site from the ground up. The project explores the darkest recesses of the nightmare, and provides users with a way to explore their own deepest fears and worst nightmares. A classic Photoshop collage design, Nightmares combines photography, illustration and typography to evoke the feeling that the viewer is living in someone else's nightmare.

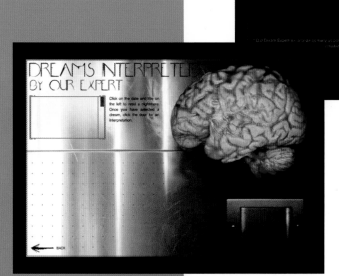

:MAKE_YOUR_SELECTION

SUBMIT YOUR NIGHTMARE

SUBMIT

CLEAR

YOUR NAME

YOUR E-MAIL

THE TITLE OF YOUR NIGHTMARE

DESCRIBE YOUR NIGHTMARE HERE - MAXIMUM OF 500 WORDS

DREAMS INTERPRETED BY OUR EXPERT

Click on the date and title on the left to read a nightmare. Once you have selected a dream, click the door for an interpretation.

BACK

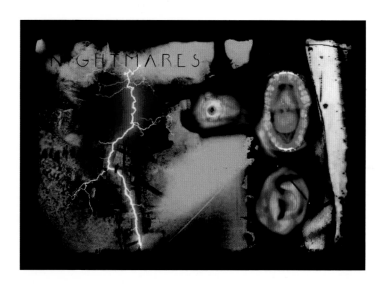

NIGHTMARES

# ANAMORPH

## Anamorph

A journey of information through multiple mediums, Anamorph serves as WDDG's motion graphics demo reel. Anamorph's purpose is to showcase the WDDG's style, approach and way of thinking. The film demonstrates WDDG's broadcast capabilities—digital media. Anamorph was shot entirely on a Sony DV cam and edited in Adobe After Effects. Layer upon layer of graphics were laid over the film, inter-acting and affecting the interaction between the cap-tured footage and motion graphics. The studio's visual approach to broadcast work is steeped in their origins in the interactive field. WDDG places great emphasis on motion graphics and its ability to enhance and extend a story or a message, which is especially evident in Anamorph.

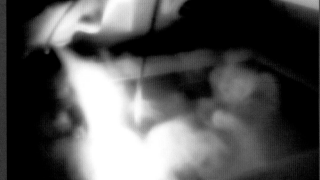

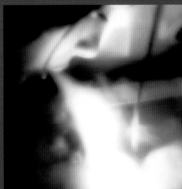

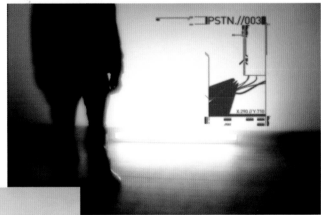

# mY pEt sKeLeTOn

Canadian artist Vincent Marcone's site features a number of stunningly dark and whimsical pieces. Marcone's work moves between the old and new worlds, mixing old-fashioned artistic techniques and legends with contemporary technologies and current affairs. "Devil" is an intaglio print created by etching textures and drawing onto a zinc metal plate, then rubbing the imprint with ink and sending it through a hand-turned press. "Struwwelpeter" is a personal piece commemorating the artist's fondness for German folklore. mY pEt sKeLeTOn was developed by focusing and merging elements from Marcone's dreams within a cyberspace designed to encourage users to explore a digital dreamscape.

**52**

AND WHEN I SAY GOOD NIGHT
THE PICTURES IN MY HEAD
WILL DANCE AROUND MY ROOM
AND FROLIC IN MY BED
AND WHEN I SAY GOOD DAY
THEY HIDE BEHIND MY EYES
WAITING FOR THE DREAMING
TO BRING THEM BACK ALIVE

"STRUWWELPETER"                  CLOSE

"CHILDREN AND WORLD HEALTH"

**Janine White** Programmer/Animation**Tristan Holmberg** Studio**mY pEt sKeLeTOn**

## The Place

54 A moody and elegant photographic animation, The Place was created by Czech designer Michal Oppitz. The old structure shown in this piece is a devastated cloister located in Cheb, in the Czech Republic. Oppitz' basic idea was to evoke the strange feelings that surround visitors as they wander through the place—every battered old wall and dusty broken window has a story to tell. Each segment features its own style of layered animation to highlight the action. Jozef Hasilla created four music loops, each designed specifically to accompany a single stage. The final composition was published on the isolate.cz website and presented as reclusion work at Oppitz' school. (Thanks to: Tomas Moscak, Lucie Svobodova, isolate.cz, VUT Faculty of Fine Arts, Brno.)

... *run down the stairs* ...

*run down the stairs*

# scrEAm taBÚ ©

Interactive portfolio Portfolio interactivo 1024x768

## scrEAm taBÚ Website

Spanish designer Rafael Ferrando Flores developed scrEAm taBÚ, an online "digital dynamical environment," to showcase his portfolio of select commercial and personal projects. In all his work, Flores attempts to express the graphical vision of his own perspectives and influences applied within different working environments and projects. Illusion and inspiration are the primary forces in Flores' work, intensifying fluidity between the elements in the design process.

56

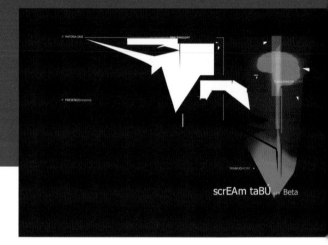

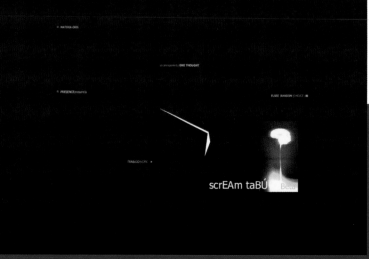

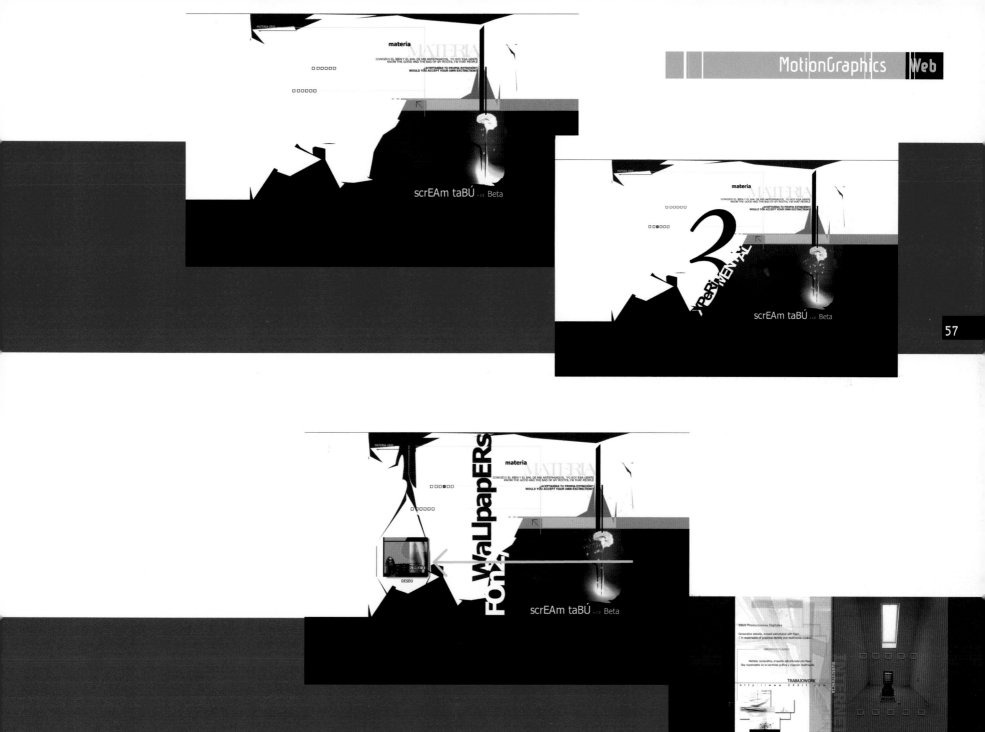

## Move Design Reel

Move Design is a visual communications design firm specializing in identity, graphic design, interaction design and motion graphics. The San Francisco based studio's motion graphics reel showcases their latest work, and employs a variety of production techniques from frame-by-frame, manually crafted sequences, to responsive, interactive and algorithmically generated animations and imagery. This piece showcases Move Design's ability to create provocative visuals that achieve a fine balance of stimulation, recognition and entertainment. The group's work is formed by their experience and deep understanding of new media development—nonlinear structures, time-based media, software programming and user interface design.

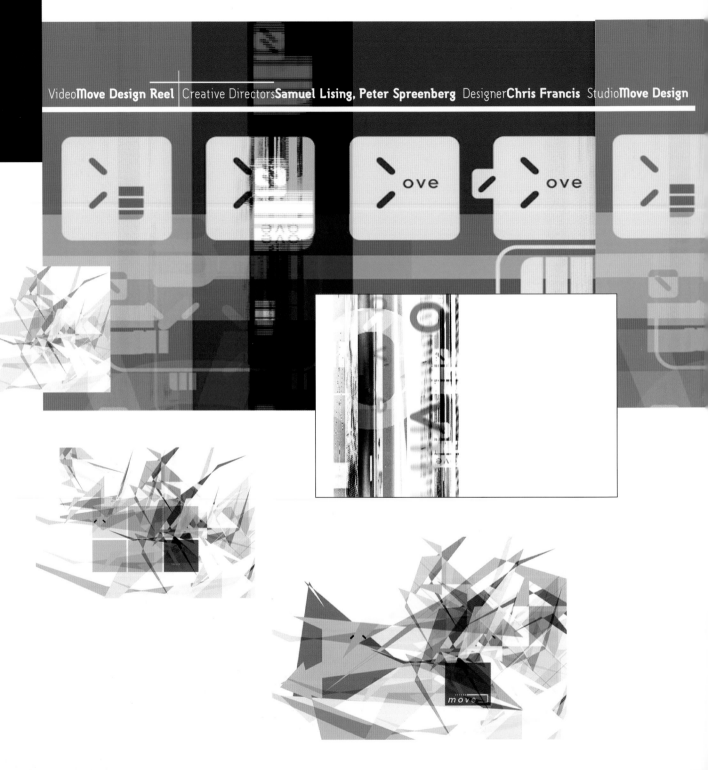

Video**Move Design Reel** | Creative Directors**Samuel Lising, Peter Spreenberg** Designer**Chris Francis** Studio**Move Design**

## I.D. Magazine: Interactive Media Design Review 2000

60

Move Design was commissioned to develop a microsite showcasing the winners of I.D. Magazine's annual Interactive Media Design competition 2000. The goal was to create a site that was user interface-intensive—affording a subtle parody of the industry. The design is rational and appropriate for a usability-sensitized audience, while slightly "over-the-top" in its delivery. The site is a custom Shockwave application that allows users to browse winning projects by category, or in a more free-form manner. Built in Macromedia Director with imported Flash assets, the website uses object-oriented programming methods to generate the motion, behavior and response of each entry, represented as graphic icons.

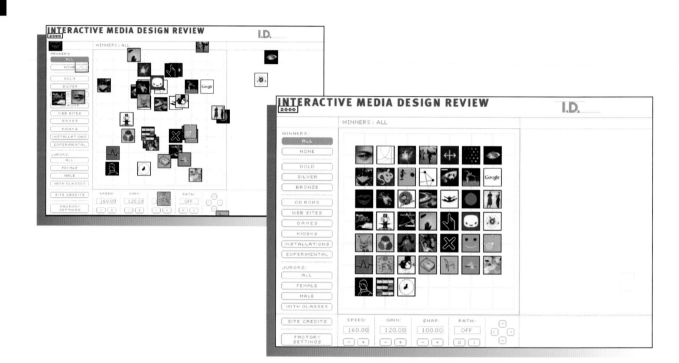

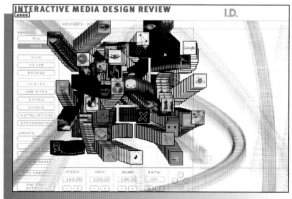

Designer**Peter Spreenberg** Studio**Move Design**

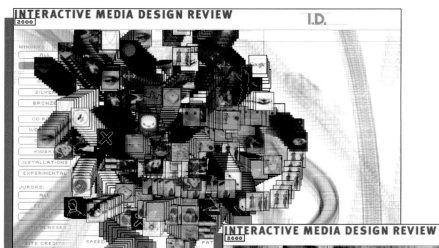

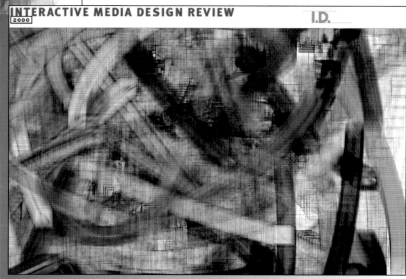

## IKDA CD-ROM

Designer Ross Mawdsley created this CD-ROM as a promotional piece for his company, IKDA. Designed for maximum impact, it needed to look sharp and stylish, while remaining extremely user-friendly. The CD is a showcase of recent work from IKDA's portfolio. The project began with sketches, with imagery built in Photoshop and Illustrator. Mawdsley moved to Flash for the final compositions, adding interactivity. As IKDA caters to a young, trendy, design-conscious market, the disc was delivered to record companies, magazines, book publishers and clothing retailers in an effort to attract new clients.

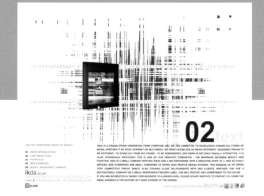

simian / splash
version1-0

GO BACK TO MENU

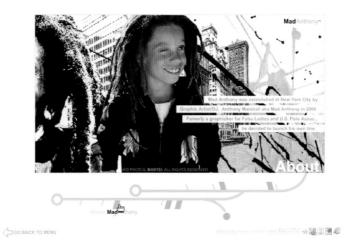

MadAnthony™

Mad Anthony was established in New York City by
Graphic Artist/DJ, Anthony Marshall aka Mad Anthony in 2000.

Fomerly a graphicker for Fubu Ladies and U.S. Polo Assoc...,
he decided to launch his own line.

KID PHOTOS: MARTEL ALL RIGHTS RESERVED

About

About **Mad**Anthony

GO BACK TO MENU

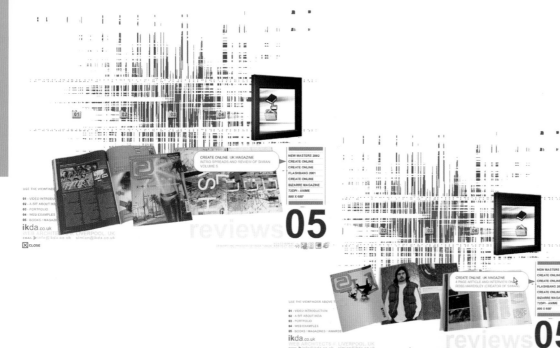

USE THE VIEWFINDER

01 - VIDEO INTRODU
02 - A BIT ABOUT
03 - PORTFOLIO
04 - WEB EXAMPLES
05 - BOOKS / MAGAZIN

ik**da**.co.uk

X CLOSE

CREATE ONLINE. UK MAGAZINE
INTRO SPREADS AND REVIEW OF SIMIAN
VOLUME 5

NEW MASTERS 2002
CREATE ONLINE
CREATE ONLINE
FLASHBANG 2001
CREATE ONLINE
BIZARRE MAGAZINE
72DPI · ANIME
800 X 600'

reviews **05**

USE THE VIEWFINDER ABOVE T

01 - VIDEO INTRODUCTION
02 - A BIT ABOUT IKDA
03 - PORTFOLIO
04 - WEB EXAMPLES
05 - BOOKS / MAGAZINES / AWARDS

ik**da**.co.uk

CREATE ONLINE. UK MAGAZINE
4 PAGE ARTICLE AND INTERVIEW ON
ROSS MAWDSLEY (CREATOR OF SIMIAN)

NEW MASTERS 2002
CREATE ONLINE
CREATE ONLINE
FLASHBANG 2001
CREATE ONLINE
BIZARRE MAGAZINE
72DPI · ANIME
800 X 600'

reviews **05**

## Simian

The Simian Project was originally set up as a creative showpiece to attract clients to Ross Mawdsley's Liverpool-based design studio, www.ikda.co.uk. Since Volume 1 was released in 1998, the concept has grown into something much bigger than a promotional show-case. The designer uses Simian as a platform of expression, trying out new ideas and styles—as a vehicle for social commentary. An ongoing personal project, Simian affords Mawdsley a forum to produce creatively, free from the con-straints artists normally encounter when working with clients.

## Tuesdae Website

Tuesdae, the singer, DJ, performer and client, asked HONEST for their help in extending her personality online. Happy to assist a favorite client, the HONEST team began work by shooting numerous photos of Tuesdae in skimpy outfits and kicky poses. The full-color images were too erotic for a family audience, and the designers decided to use her silhouette image instead. The primary goal was to have fun designing the site, which in turn would make it fun for the audience to use. Going with a "Charlie's Angels-disco-007-funkified-psychedelic-techno-rave-girl power" theme, HONEST created a colorful, kitschy site to show off the entertainer's considerable assets.

TUESDAE

POP!

girlfinder

TUESDAE

Stereo show

girlfinder

TUESDAE

guest list

**Fridays: GBH (Great British House)**
Centro-Fly, 45 West 21 Street (between 5 & 6 Ave.)
$10 reduced
Print out this page or call 212-539-3858

FLICKFIX

fan club

DJ show by Tuesdae, performing live on stage.
I sing my own tracks at various points during my set.
Just two turntables and a wireless headset microphone.

WebsiteAmerican Dream | DesignerRatsi Studio/PhotoNouchema SoundSynchrone, Ratsi

## American Dream

The American Dream was created by the French design collective eMovie. The Flash project features grayscale photographs of urban elements mixed with colorful graphic images. Additional sound loops were incorporated to create an overall experience of syncopated visuals and music to entertain the viewer. eMovie demonstrates how their diverse skills and creative experiences entice contemporary audiences.

68

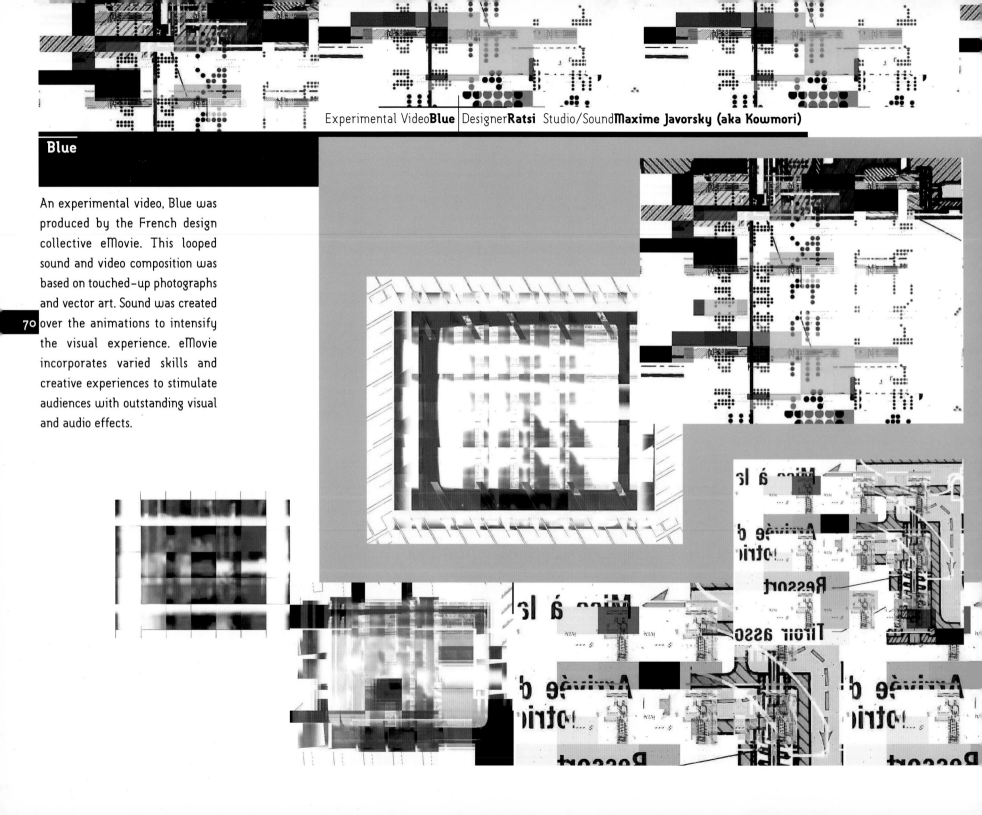

Experimental Video**Blue** | Designer**Ratsi**  Studio/Sound**Maxime Javorsky (aka Kowmori)**

## Blue

An experimental video, Blue was produced by the French design collective eMovie. This looped sound and video composition was based on touched-up photographs and vector art. Sound was created over the animations to intensify the visual experience. eMovie incorporates varied skills and creative experiences to stimulate audiences with outstanding visual and audio effects.

70

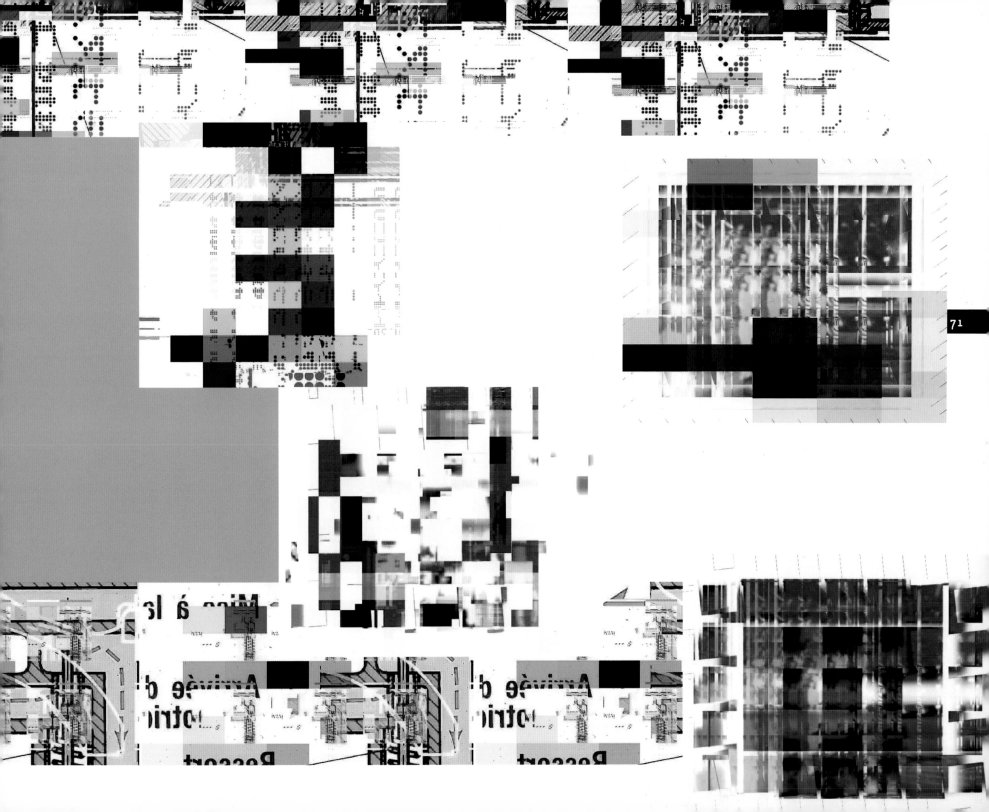

## Factory

Factory was created by the French design collective eMovie. It was produced in Flash animation and was developed by manipulating still and moving images. The concept was to capture the physical and human elements of a factory environment. The Paris based group of artists also showcase their talents by creating unique VJ/DJ performances, visually effective websites and stimulating videos with their fresh concepts.

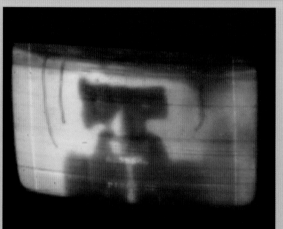

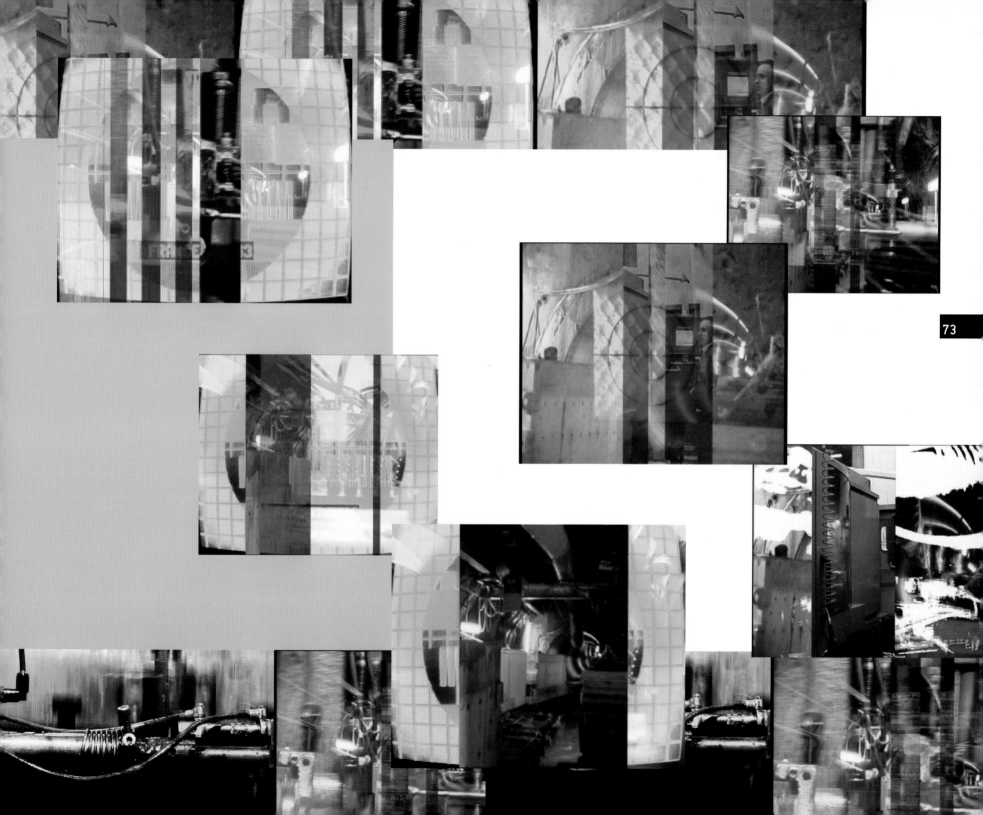

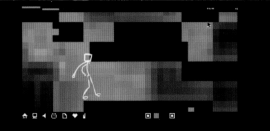

# eMovie Website Intro

French design collective eMovie, develops artistic visual material for multimedia applications. They designed the website introduction to showcase their diverse talents in experimental video, cartoons, sound and graphic design. Neon, the wire character and main orchestrator of the eMovie collective, presents the eMovie vision. The Paris based group of artists also showcase their talents by creating unique user interface experiences.

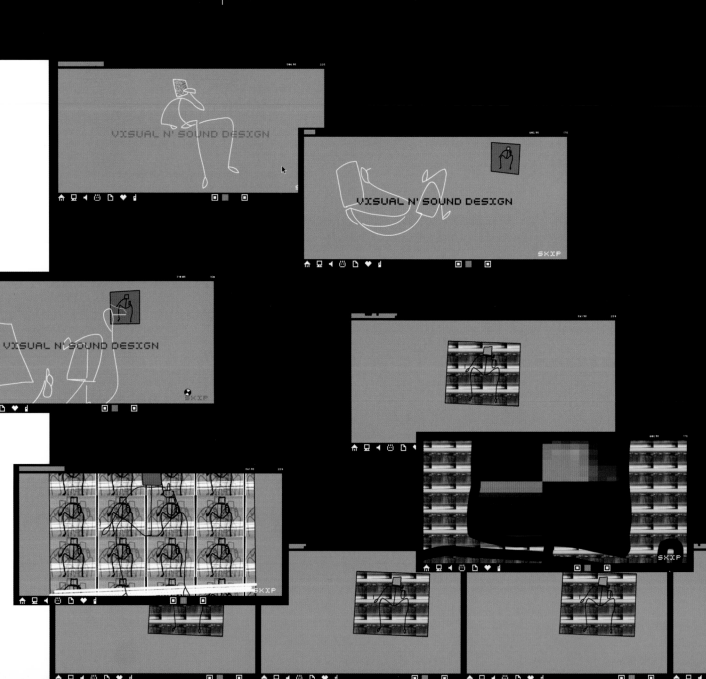

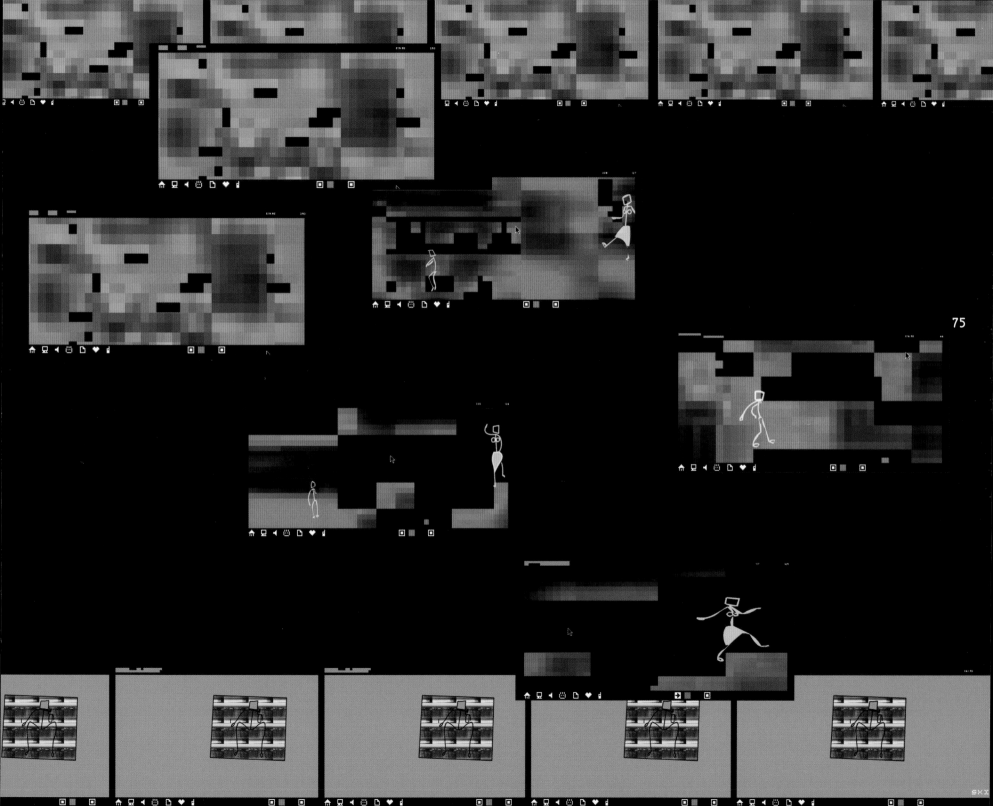

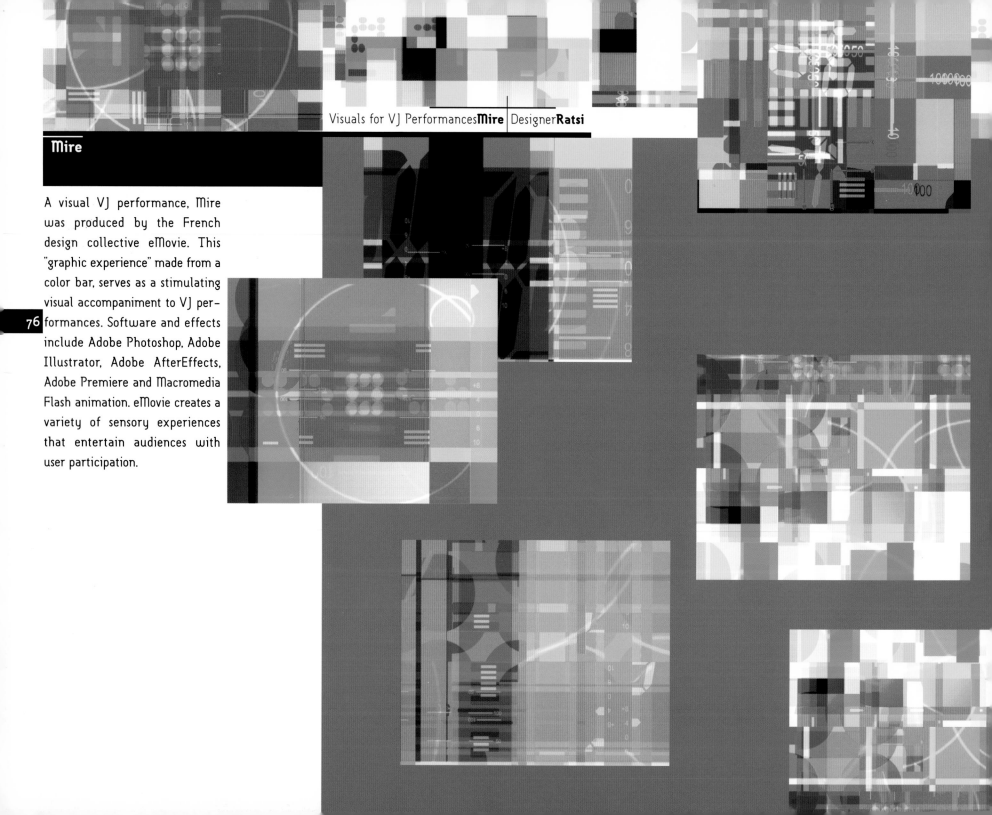

Visuals for VJ Performances**Mire** | Designer**Ratsi**

# Mire

A visual VJ performance, Mire was produced by the French design collective eMovie. This "graphic experience" made from a color bar, serves as a stimulating visual accompaniment to VJ performances. Software and effects include Adobe Photoshop, Adobe Illustrator, Adobe AfterEffects, Adobe Premiere and Macromedia Flash animation. eMovie creates a variety of sensory experiences that entertain audiences with user participation.

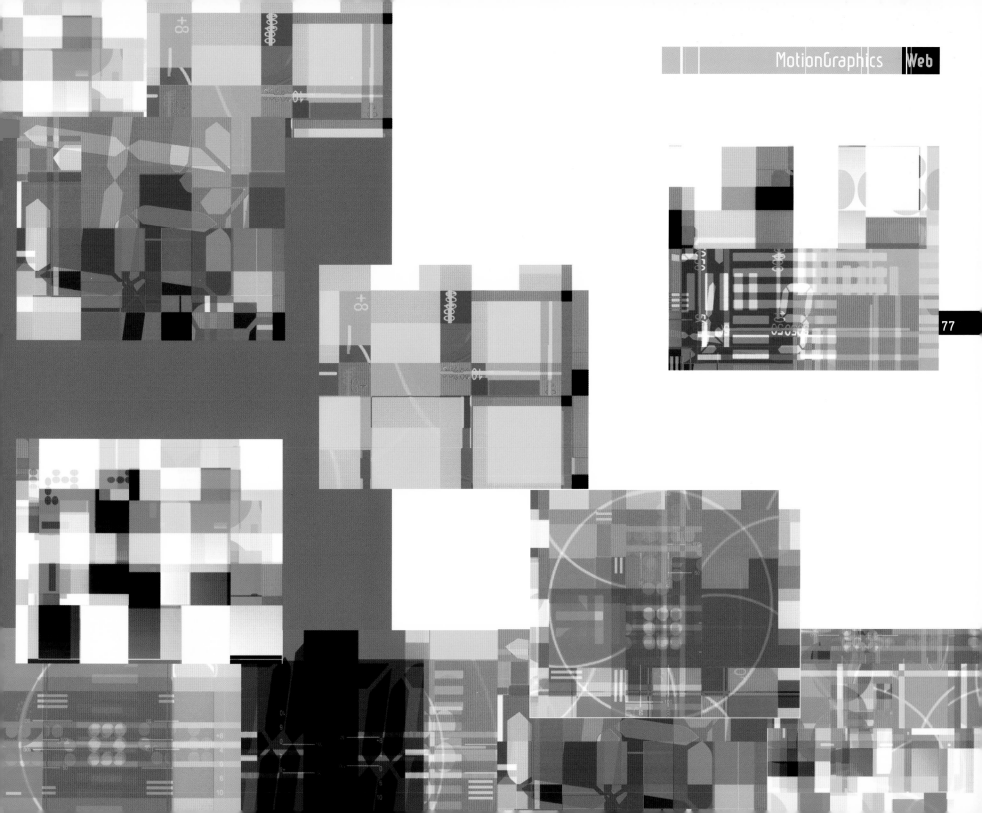

## Nebula

An experimental video, Nebula was created by the French design collective eMovie. This looped sound and video composition was based on digitally manipulated photographs. Sound **78** was created over the animations to enhance the visual experience. The Paris based group of artists also showcase their many talents by creating unique VJ/DJ performances for the Euro-music scene.

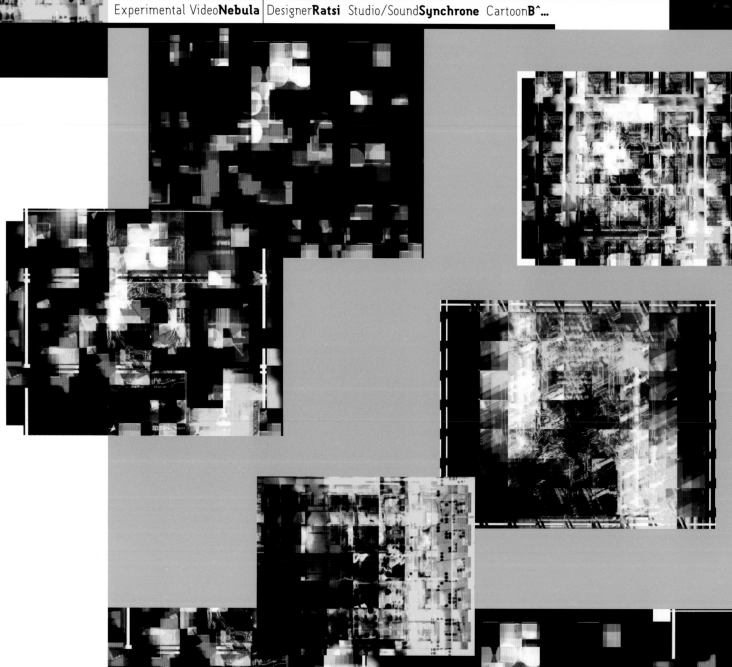

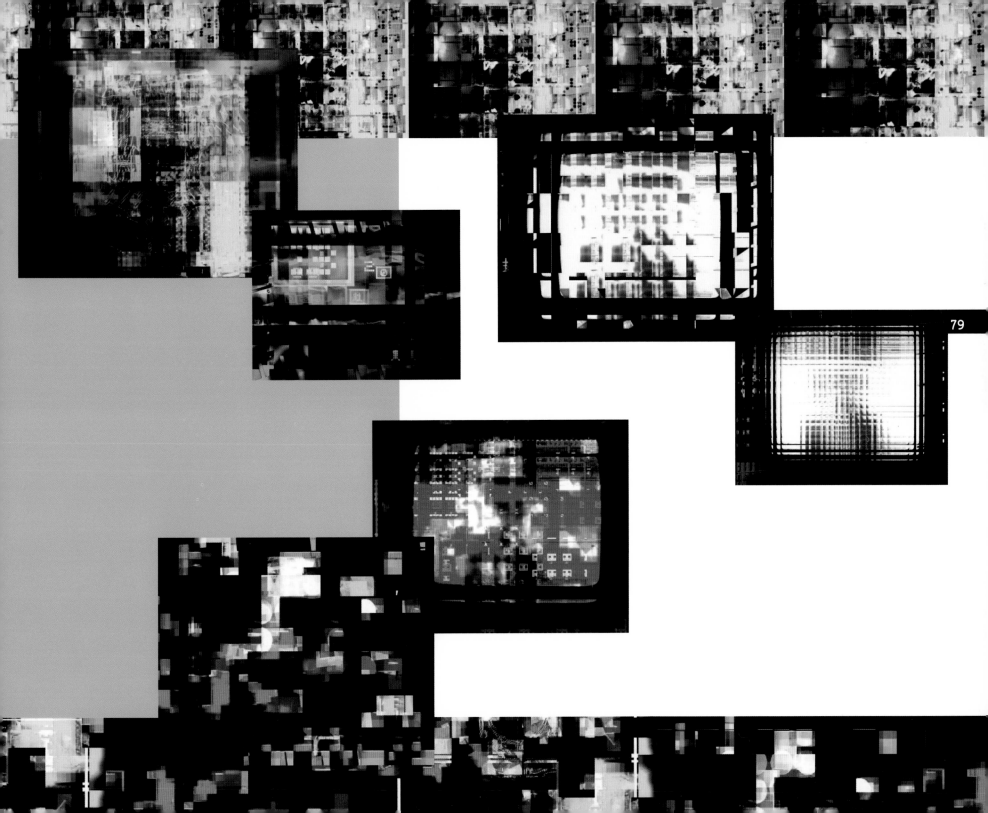

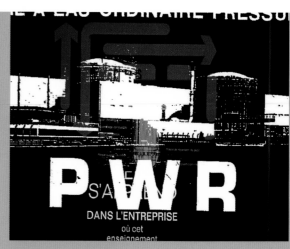

**80** An exciting visual VJ performance, PWR was created by the French design collective eMovie. eMovie's graphic rendition on the theme of "energy" adds visual excitement to the VJ experience. A conglomerate of typography and visuals were assembled in Adobe Photoshop, Adobe Illustrator, Adobe AfterEffects, Adobe Premiere and Macromedia Flash animation. eMovie creates a variety of sensory experiences that entertain audiences with user participation.

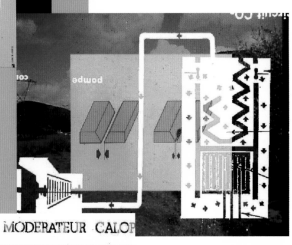

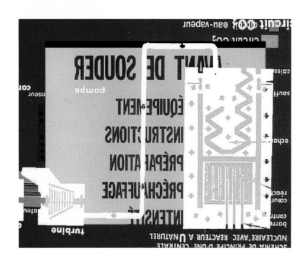

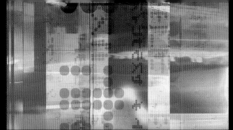

# Red

Red was designed by the French collective eMovie. A spectrum of graphic Flash animations were produced from still photography combined with brilliantly colored vector and bitmap art. Waves of colorful tones move in rhythmic patterns. eMovie specializes in multimedia techniques in videography, photography, cartoon imagery, VJing, DJing, compositing, image and sound sampling.

82

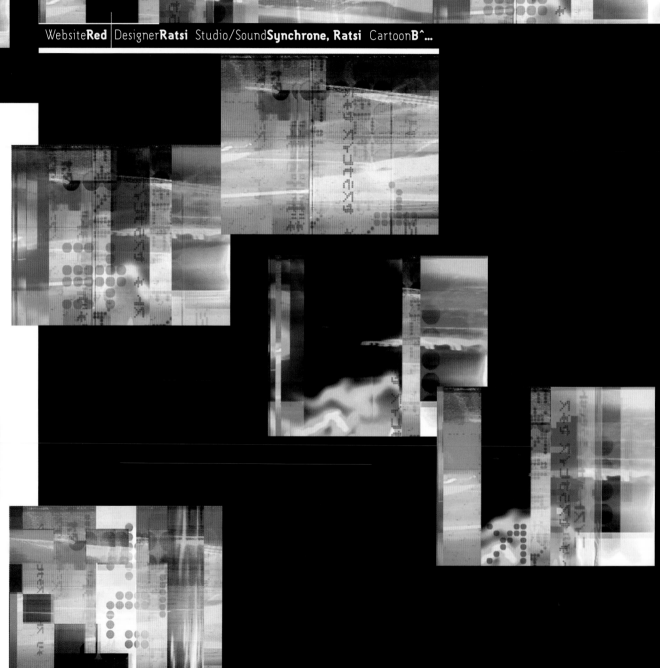

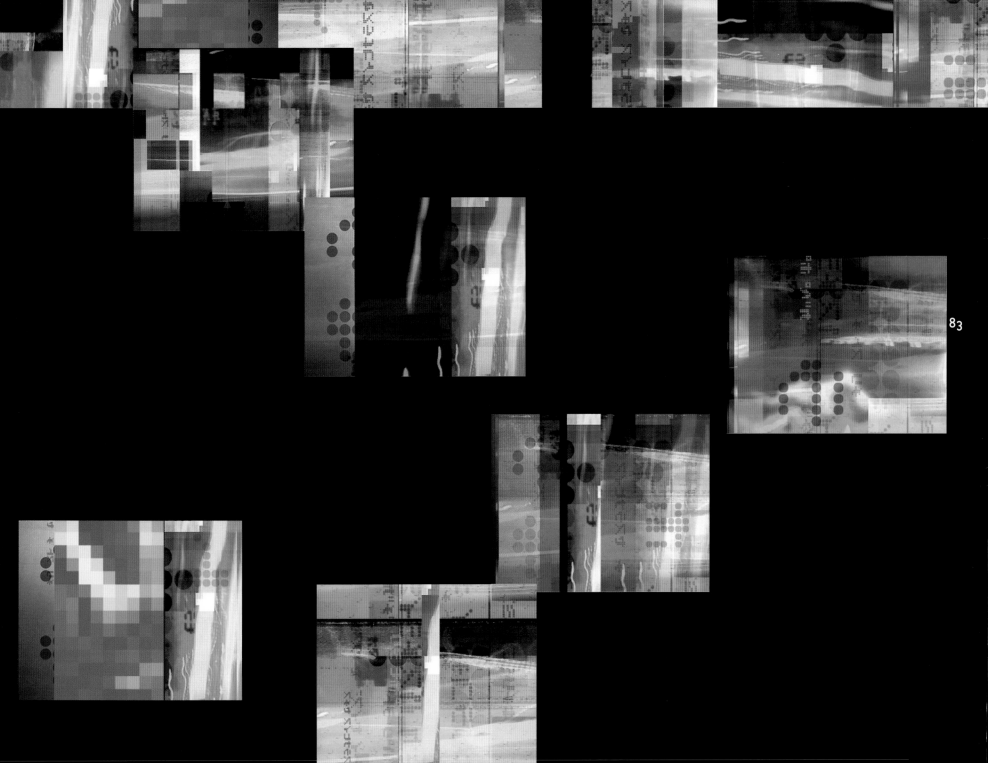

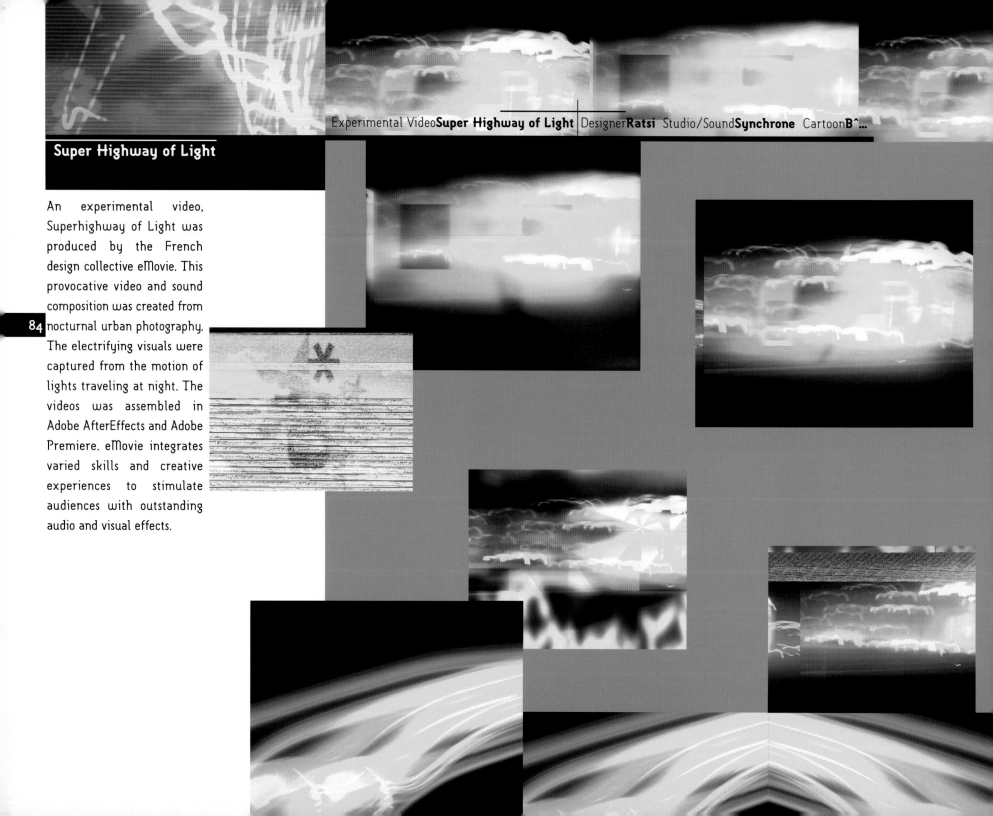

## Super Highway of Light

An experimental video, Superhighway of Light was produced by the French design collective eMovie. This provocative video and sound composition was created from nocturnal urban photography. The electrifying visuals were captured from the motion of lights traveling at night. The videos was assembled in Adobe AfterEffects and Adobe Premiere. eMovie integrates varied skills and creative experiences to stimulate audiences with outstanding audio and visual effects.

84

**Baroque**

Video Game**Baroque** | Creative Director**Chris Do** Designer/Animator**Jessie Huang, Chris Do, Vanessa Marzaroli** Studio**BL:ND**

An array of subtly shifting typefaces blend together to reveal hidden meanings and conjure the mystery of the Sega game. The aim was to tease the viewer into a realm of fantasy and discovery. In undertaking the project, the BL:ND team was presented with the unique opportunity of creating the game's complex graphic environment simultaneously with the designer's development of the characters and sets. The sequence was created entirely in Adobe After Effects using both scanned material and original smoke footage shot on 35mm.

## Circus2K1

New York based designer Carlo Vega's developed Circus 2K1 for Graffodisiak, his personal site. Vega's inspiration for his artwork typically comes from everyday life. This project was the designer's social commentary on power, risks taking and the way people put on masks, all put together with a twist. Circus 2K1 was one of Vega's early experiments with friction and velocity, controlling movement only with action scripting. The post-modern studies Vega creates for Graffodisiak are exclusively personal. Vega's goals are to express feelings in constructive ways, pushing the boundaries of design as he continues to evolve as an artist.

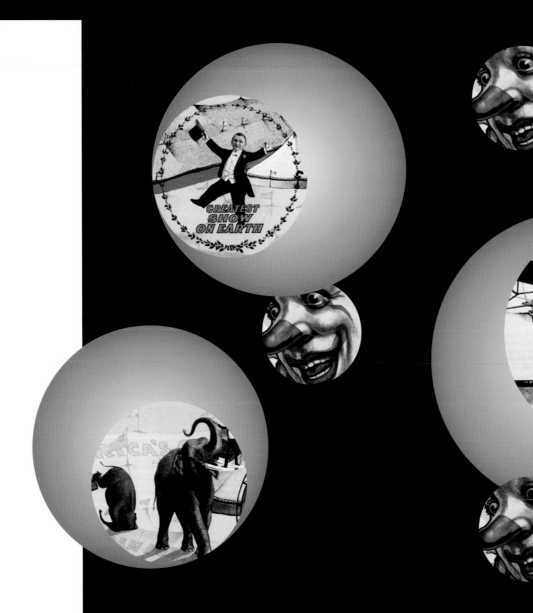

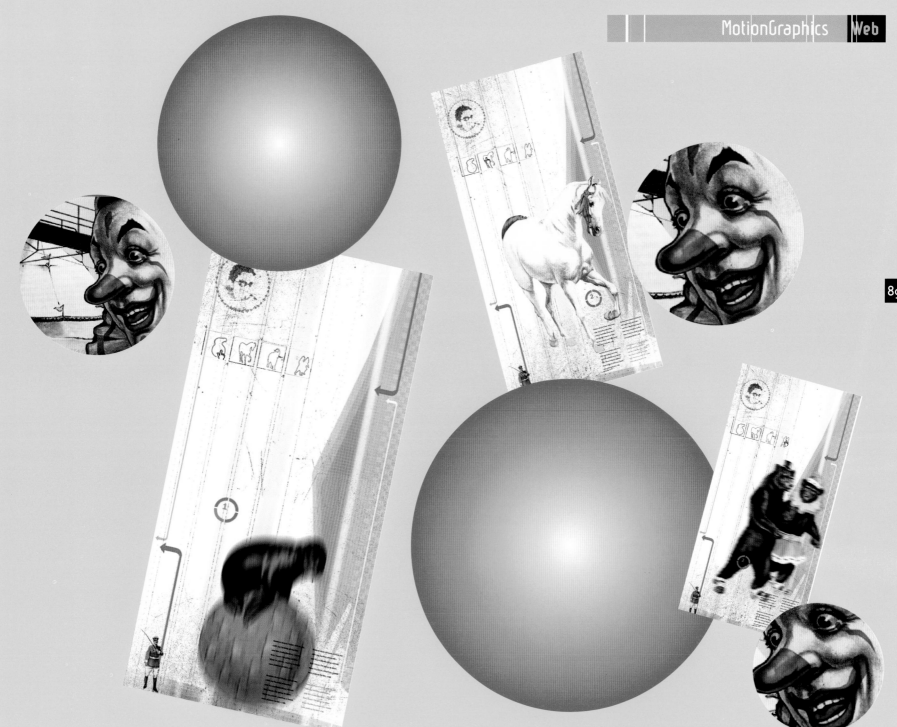

## M.O.P. Music Video

Chris Brown created a Flash music video for the rap group M.O.P. The popular band was looking for the same high energy and visual effects found in broadcast music videos, yet contained within a file size that is easily viewable over the web. The designer used Adobe After Effects to crop and manipulate the video footage, importing image sequences into Flash to animate and sync to the song. Since file size did become a major issue, Brown decided to present the footage as a video wall, allowing him to crop sequences significantly smaller than the 600x300 window. The resulting work beautifully showcases M.O.P.'s contemporary sound, raw energy and powerful visual appeal.

# ifilm
## ifilm.com

Station I.D. on ifilm.com **Ifilm Pre-Roll 2** | Designer**Chris Brown** Studio**Ifilm**

## Ifilm Pre-Roll 2

Chris Brown from cboogie was asked to develop an energetic Station I.D. for ifilm.com. This project's concept called for building a high-energy vector-based pre-roll with the Ifilm logo twirling into the frame. The designer relied on duplicating animated movie clips of each letter in the Ifilm logo, as well as a series of overlapping masks for the background. Brown feels that using static images in motion evokes a cinematic experience that is both appealing and accessible on the web. Constantly challenged by the limitations of file size and processor speed, the designer thrives on experimenting with innovative ways of overcoming these obstacles.

## Ifilm Pre-Roll 1

San Francisco designer Chris Brown's assignment was to create an animated "station I.D." to play in front of short films on the ifilm.com website. This pre-roll was designed to emulate analog film running through a jittery projector. Brown experimented with animating a series of duplicate Ifilm logos flying over each other and exploding out of the frame. The frantic piece succeeds in capturing and keeping the audience's attention, prepping viewers for the unique experience of the upcoming film.

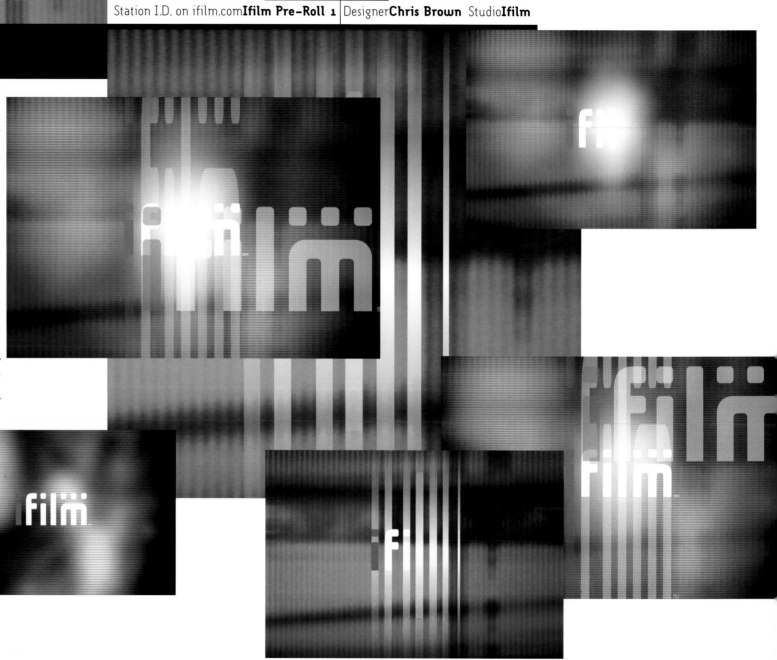

## Let's Entertain

"Let's Entertain: Life's Guilty Pleasures" was an art exhibition mounted by the Walker Art Center. General Working Group was commissioned by Andrew Blauvelt, the Walker's Design Director, to design a motion graphic entry feature for the show. Walker's criteria asked that the piece speak to celebrity, desire, seduction and transgression; the "spectacularization" of everyday experience. The San Francisco-based studio designed a projection that lists the names of the artists and the show title in moving and morphing typography set within a human heart, visualizing a collapse of the traditional "mind/body" split.

**96**

## Hypnerotomachia Poliphili

This immersive media installation, a creation of San Francisco's General Working Group, was inspired by the Renaissance book "Hypnerotomachia Poliphili", published in Venice in 1499. The text is a polyglot, a concatenation of dream-within-dream narrative interwoven with scholarly treatises. A story driven by desire and sensuous engagement with the imaginary and symbolic realms. This project re-examines the questions posed by the enigmatic book. The artwork integrates augmented reality with video, three-dimensional sound, music, typography and poetry in an immersive, interactive environment. This work-in-progress provokes users to redefine the relationship between their bodily sensory experience with symbolic realms.

StudioGeneral Working Group

TITVDINE DEGLI AMANT
E AMOROSE PVELLE LA N
VNDAMENTE DECHIAR
MEDAGLI DII AMATE.ET
TICANTANTI VIDE.

CVNOMAIDITANT
uio aptamente fe accommoda
nani difertando copiofo &

## American Center for Design – New Media, New Narratives

San Francisco's General Working Group was called upon to create conference graphics for the American Center for Design. Using the elements and research involved in the creation of the New Media, New Narratives event poster, word inquiries were made into a large database of literary texts. The results were then reprocessed and resubmitted through the database and several comparative algorithms. These passages, along with the characters from the poster, became the basis for the visual representation and sound of the project. The final expression was rendered out to video and edited to loop seamlessly. The work was projected onto a large screen for viewing.

**100**

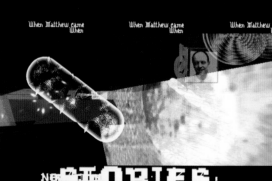

R. Paul Seymour with Gail Swanlund and Akira Rabelais  Studio**General Working Group**

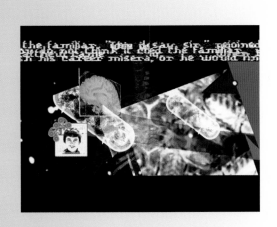

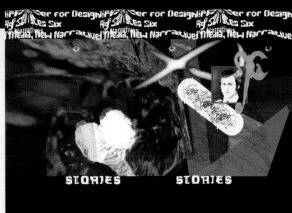

## Formsmart

The foundation for Martin Hesselmeier's formsmart project was completely experimental. The German artist focused on the idea of changing the design using random activities available in new media applications. The base visual elements of the experimental artwork remain the same, but are changed by the random shifting of the x and y positions and scaling of the objects. Hesselmeier began the project by experimenting with random functions in Flash, then built the shapes that formed the basis of his creation. Every user sees a newly-generated view, which changes over time.

102

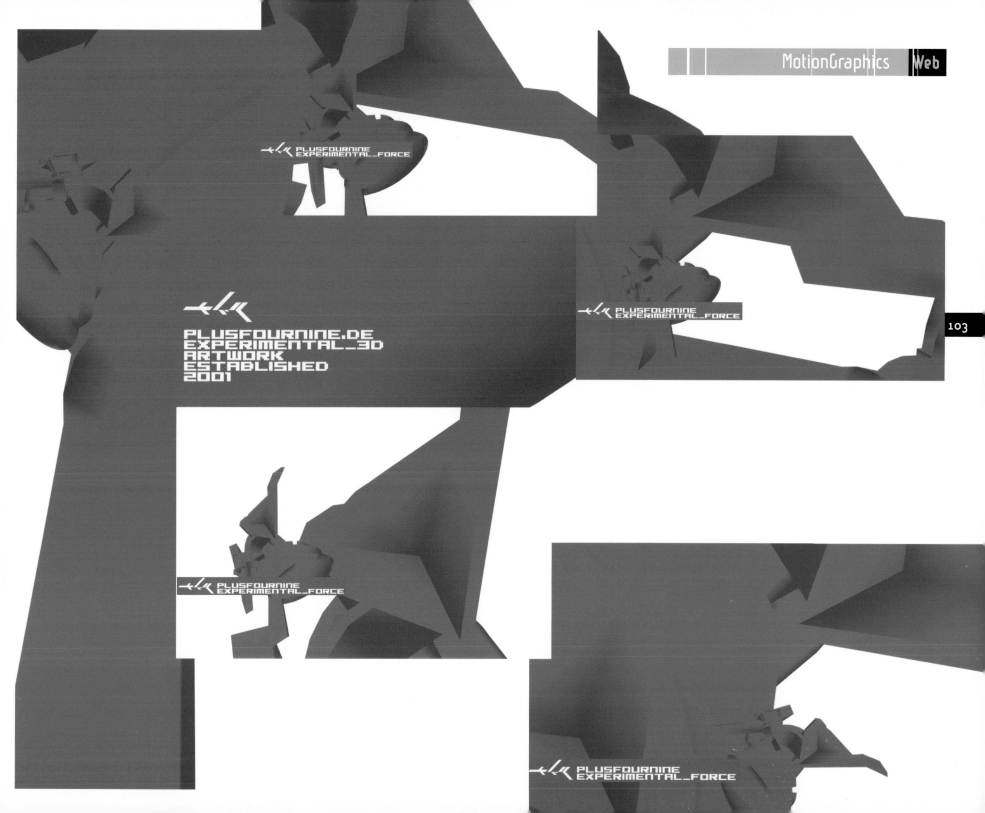

PLUSFOURNINE.DE
EXPERIMENTAL_3D
ARTWORK
ESTABLISHED
2001

## Yobun No 49

During the winter of 2000, German designer Martin Hesselmeier worked in New York City, the place that inspired Yobun No 49. Stimulated by his incredible experience there, and the open-minded people he worked with, Hesselmeier set out to chronicle his time spent in NYC. One morning while walking to work camera in hand, he took a number of interesting photographs of the environment. He then combined the images with colorful vector art and clean typography. The resulting series of scenes, interactively moving from one place to another, depict a very different view of an everyday journey in life.

PARTS OF THE
BRIDGE
CONNECTING
MANHATTAN AND
BROOKLYN

PROJECT > BROOKLYN ⇄ MANHATTAN

WALK
OVER
THE
WILLIAMSBURG
BRIDGE

IT'S MONDAY IN NYC. THE SUN IS
SHINING AND I'M WALKING OVER THE
BRIDE. THE WILLIAMSBURGBRIDE,
TO MANHATTAN.
THIS IS A REVIEW OF WHAT I SAW AND
RECOGNIZED ON THIS TRIP.
USE THE NAVIGATION ON THE LEFT.

PROJECT > BROOKLYN ⇄ MANHATTAN

WALK
OVER
THE
WILLIAMSBURG
BRIDGE

IT'S MONDAY IN NYC. THE SUN IS
SHINING AND I'M WALKING OVER THE
BRIDE. THE WILLIAMSBURGBRIDE,
TO MANHATTAN.
THIS IS A REVIEW OF WHAT I SAW AND
RECOGNIZED ON THIS TRIP.
USE THE NAVIGATION ON THE LEFT.

NO TRUCKS
OVER
THE
WILLIAMSBURG
BRIDGE

PARTS OF THE
BRIDGE
CONNECTING
MANHATTAN AND
BROOKLYN

PROJECT > BROOKLYN → MANHATTAN

WALK
OVER
THE
WILLIAMSBURG
BRIDGE

IT'S MONDAY IN NYC. THE SUN
SHINING AND I'M WALKING OVER
BRIDE. THE WILLIAMSBURGBRI
TO MANHATTAN.
THIS IS A REVIEW OF WHAT I
RECOGNIZED ON THIS TRIP.
USE THE NAVIGATION ON THE

J-TRAIN
MARCY STREET - DELANCY AVENUE
BKLYN                    MANHATTAN

PAR
BRIDGE
CONNECTING
MANHATTAN AND
BROOKLYN

DELANCY AVENUE
MANHATTAN

105

ICKS

MSBURG

GO AND SEE
HTTP://WWW.PLUSFOURNINE.DE
GET MORE 3DIMENSIONAL VIEWS
PROJECT:BKLYN->MANHATTAN

## The System

The System was inspired by a graffiti sketch book belonging to designer Sean Donohue and two close friends in the summer of 1993. The project combines brilliantly-colored vector art and Goth-style typography with grayscale bitmap images of modern imagery including automobile tires, bricks and heavy equipment. One of the experiments showcased on Donohue's personal site, Goingonsix.com, The System, asks the viewer to navigate through the image sequences, creating their own segues with the click of the mouse.

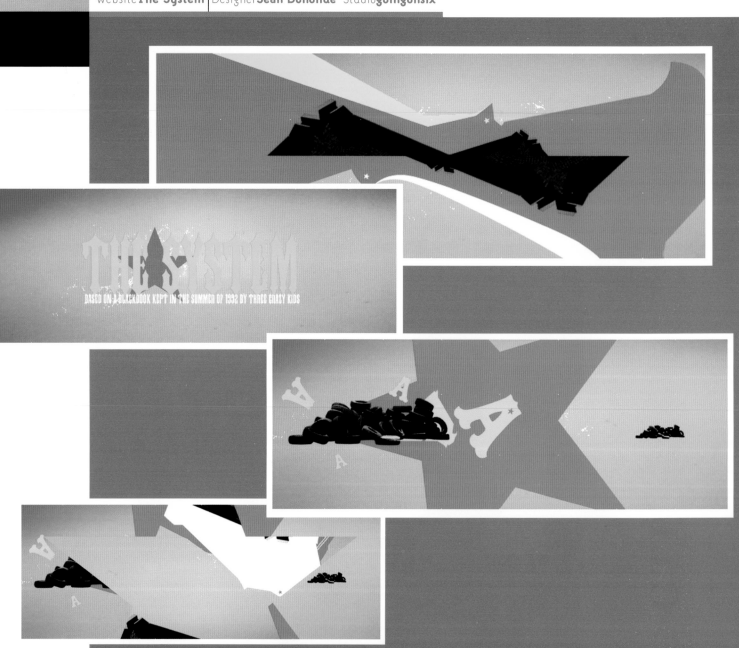

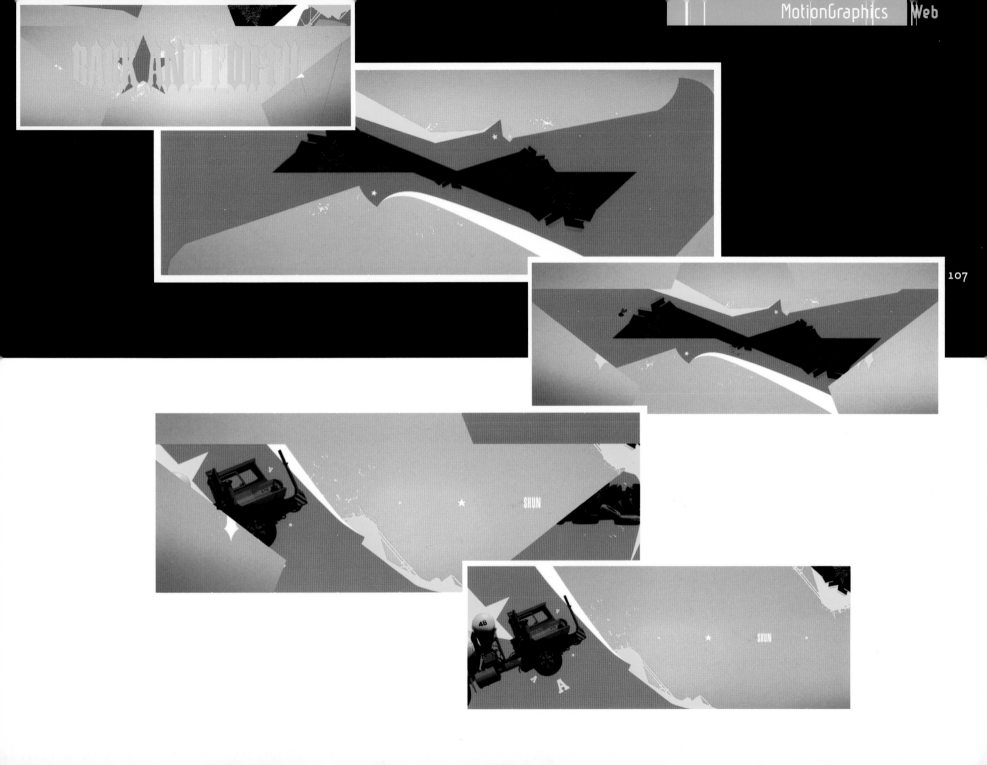

## The Diver

Goingonsix.com is Sean Donohue's personal journal site—a playground for the designer's exploration of narrative through motion graphics and interactivity. The Diver is a project inspired by Donohue's good friend, Jemma Gura (http://www.prate.com), whose "alternate reality" places her on an oil rig, working as an industrial diver, in the middle of the Pacific Ocean. Donohue's mixture of murky blue backgrounds and stark white text provide an eerie path for the diver's viewer-controlled journey through her underwater world.

**108**

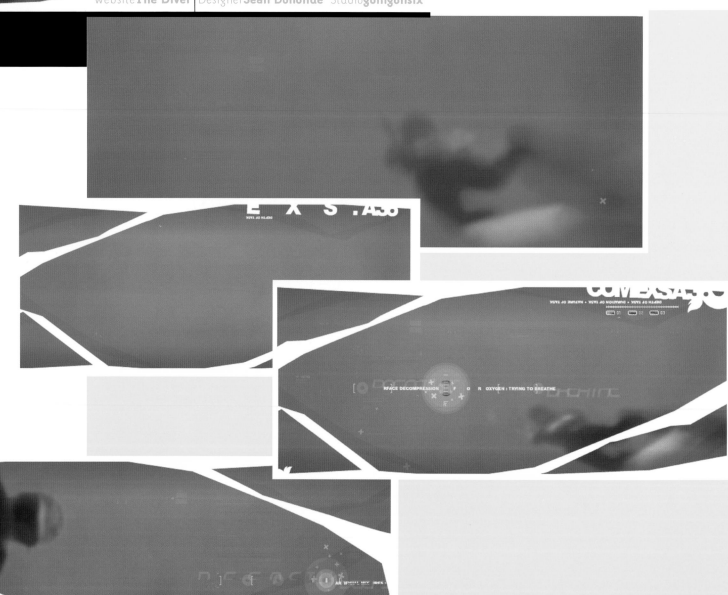

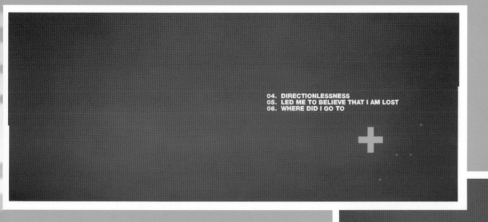

04. DIRECTIONLESSNESS
05. LED ME TO BELIEVE THAT I AM LOST
06. WHERE DID I GO TO

07. WHERE WAS I
08. WHEN I WAS OUT OF CONTROL
09. THIS ONE'S ME

10. GOTTA BE MY OWN

**33_1/3_RPM**

**33-1/3**

Apt5a designer Andy Schaaf created 33-1/3 as an experiment in photo-sequential animation combined with turntable music. The project's title was taken from the standard rotation speed at which a 12" record transmits sound at its intended pitch. The photos forming the foundation of 33-1/3 were taken in sequence while Schaaf walked home from the office. The beats in the soundtrack were lifted from the dirt-style records Schaaf uses to practice "skratching" techniques, with cuts recorded directly from the turntable to the computer. 33-1/3 was created for Schaaf's personal site, elimin8.net, as part of a project he developed for the May 1st Reboot at design portal threeoh.com.

DON"T HOLD THE BEATS BACK

**Scan**

London-based design studio D-Fuse developed the short film, "Scan," as an experiment with type to explore boundaries and dimensions. Interest in the relationship between sight and sound led D-Fuse to their creative heights, developing club visuals and installations throughout Europe—touring and exhibiting their unique imagery with musicians such as Scanner and Leftfield. Based on the theme, "Fun with Type" in the Scan project, D-Fuse used electric color and exciting motion set to mood music by Scanner, to form a hypnotic display of their multimedia prowess.

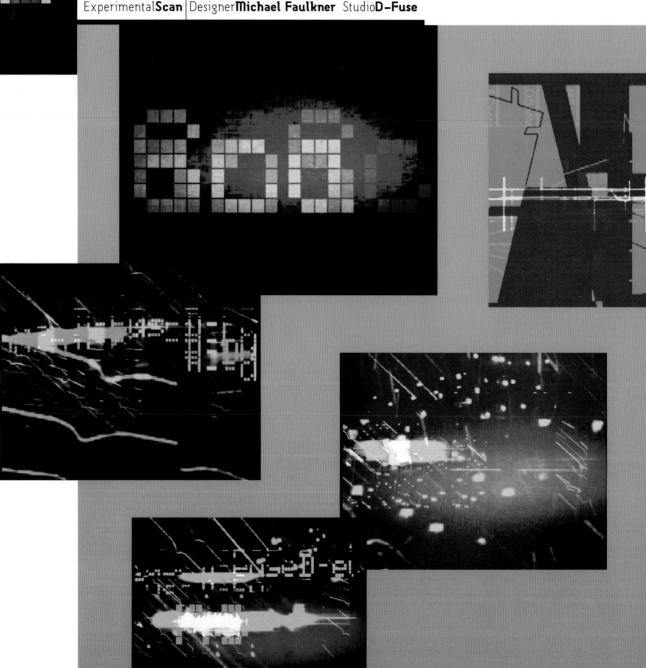

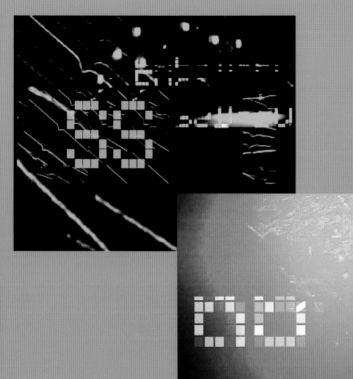

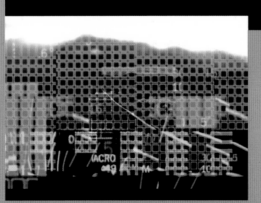

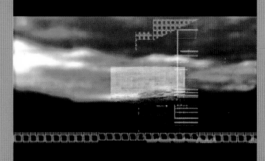

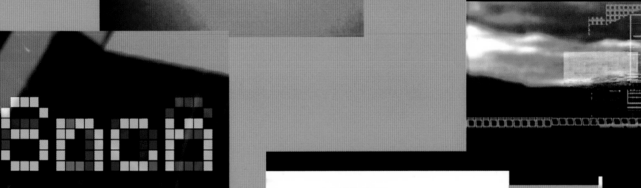

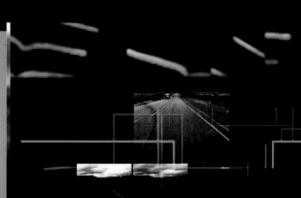

## Crash Intro 2

**114**

Crash Intro 2 is a personal online experience site designed by the French multimedia artist Lokiss. In this site, he tries to delete "web stereotypes" with a random variation of stimulating motion graphic sequences, that result in explosive effects and primary colors coupled with block style typography. The French designer's current work deals with randomness—how the perception of reality is distorted as described in the chaos theory.

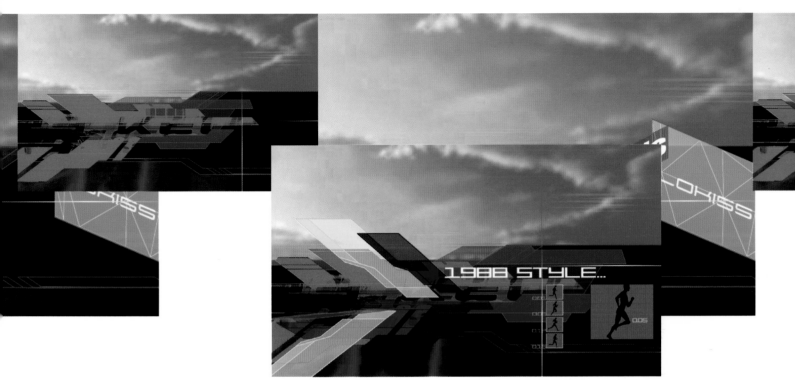

1988 STYLE...

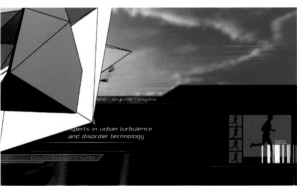

...ere · anytime · anyone

...perts in urban turbulence
and disorder technology

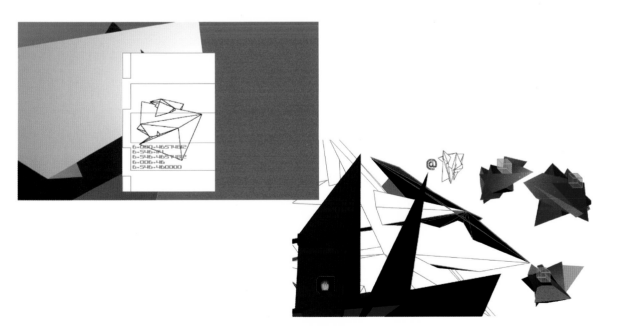

6-080-465-482
6-546-441
6-546-465-482
6-006-46
6-546-460000

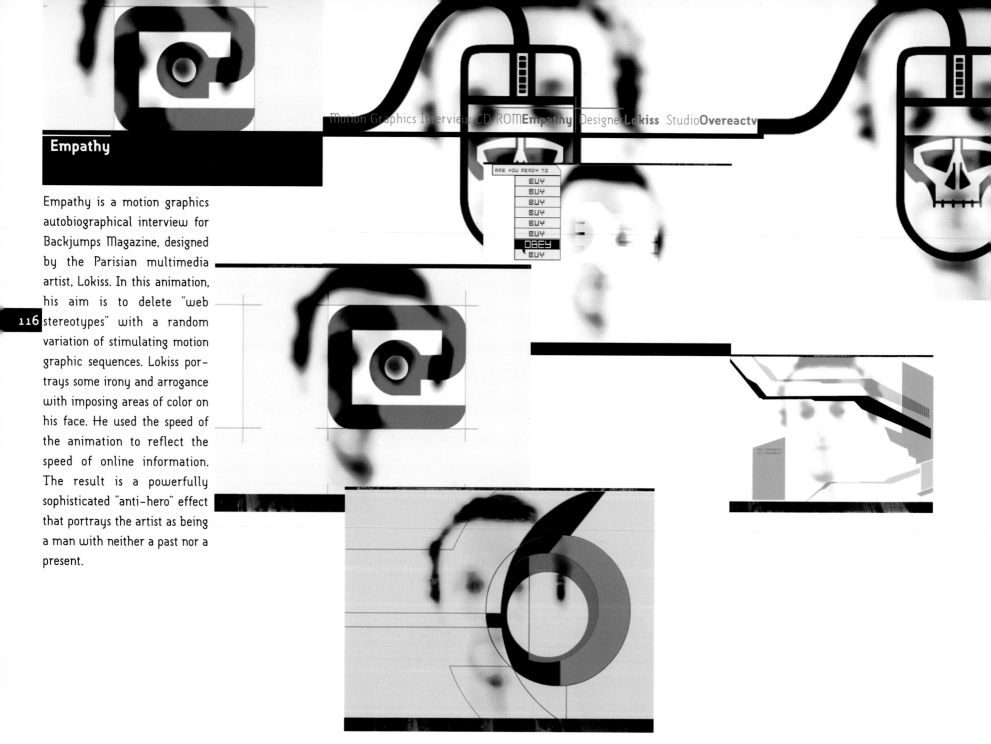

## Empathy

Empathy is a motion graphics autobiographical interview for Backjumps Magazine, designed by the Parisian multimedia artist, Lokiss. In this animation, his aim is to delete "web stereotypes" with a random variation of stimulating motion graphic sequences. Lokiss portrays some irony and arrogance with imposing areas of color on his face. He used the speed of the animation to reflect the speed of online information. The result is a powerfully sophisticated "anti-hero" effect that portrays the artist as being a man with neither a past nor a present.

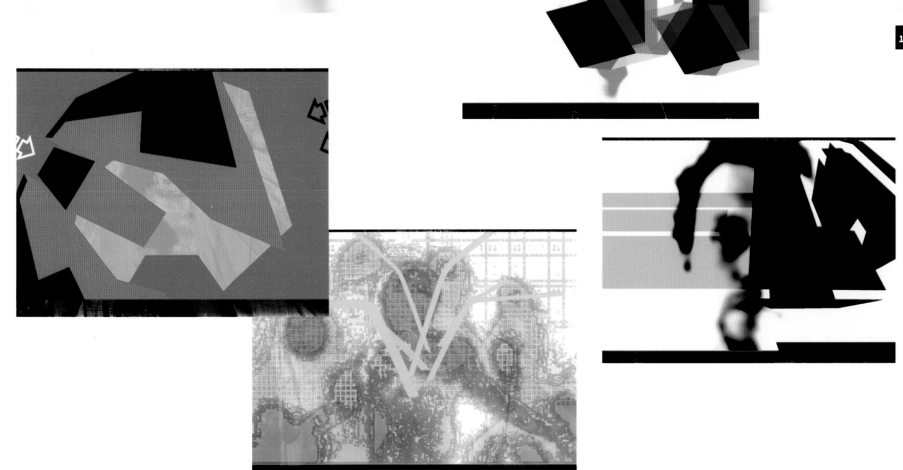

## Overeactive

118 Overeactive is a personal experience movie designed by French multimedia artist Lokiss. The vibrant, virtual graphics display soft figures in motion against a background of harsh red and black. Overeactive is an expression of oversexed excessive activity. This movie will be transformed into a new website called Pornografux. Constantly intrigued by human identity, social mass and individual loss, Lokiss continues to develop online exhibitions designed to entice a diverse global audience into experimenting with new media in new venues.

I-AM-LOKISS-2000

OVERBACTIVE

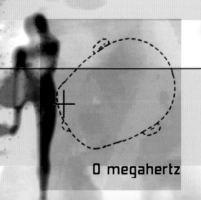

0 megahertz

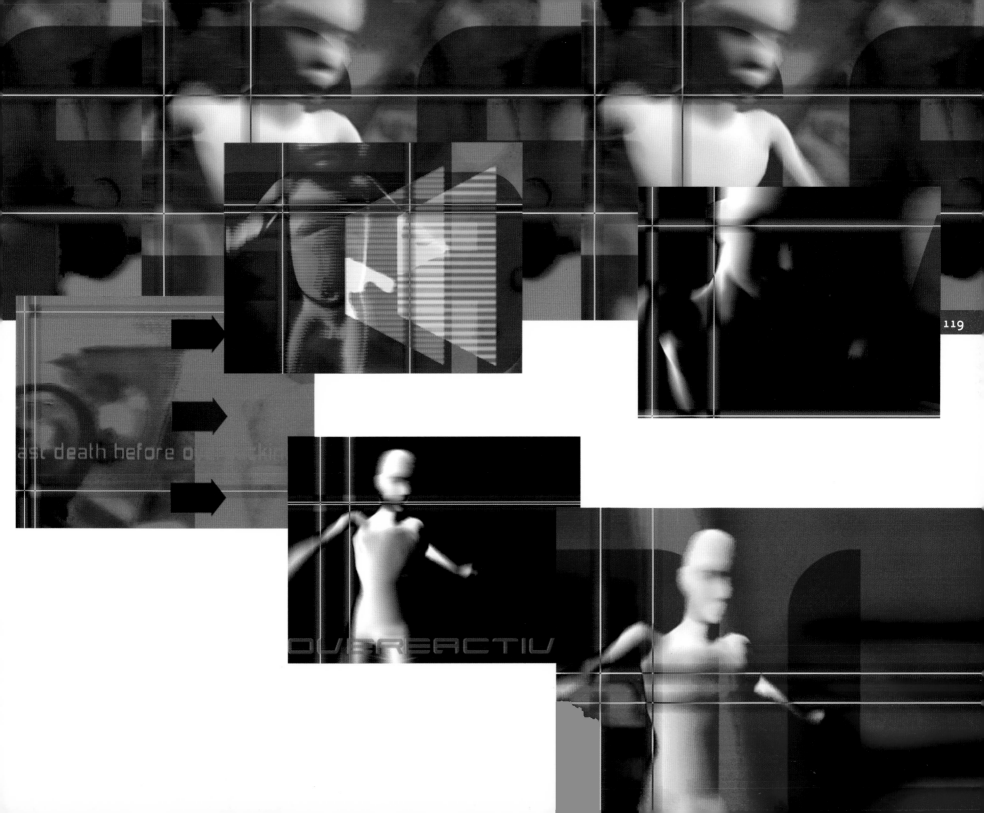

## Graffiti Dance – The Birth

**120**

Graffiti Dance – The Birth, is an experimental website designed by multimedia Paris-based artist, Lokiss. The concept was inspired by a wall painted by the artist. A group of Parisian dancers decided to create a choreography based on the mural. Then the artist transformed the filmed figures into a motion graphics mural. Through the interaction of the rhythmic dancers, Lokiss captured the essence of the movement like a graffiti dance of "rebirth". The multimedia works by French artist Lokiss are the result of his personal research into sculpture and murals.

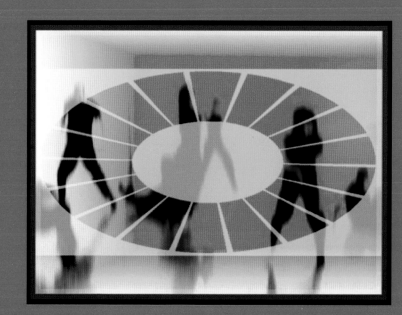

## By The Row

By The Row, designed by multimedia Paris-based artist, Lokiss, was an online experimental website. The graphic sequences begin with colorful cubist constructions that merge monochromatic compositions. The flow of images evolve into the red shadow of a man superimposed with "pixel is a virus" across his eyes. Intermingled with a variety of techniques and effects, By The Row was created with Adobe AfterEffects, Adobe Photoshop, Adobe Illustrator and Macromedia Flash. The French designer's current work deals with the perception of distorted reality.

## Specimen 22

The Specimen series, created for the artist's website, encompasses more than 100 designs from Garage Media's Ryan Klak. The concept started as a conceit, in that Klak could quickly and randomly produce pieces that other designers would spend hours creating. In Specimen 22, Klak was trying to generate the old "RayGun" style design. It symbolizes the duality of man and the utter boredom that web design is today.

124

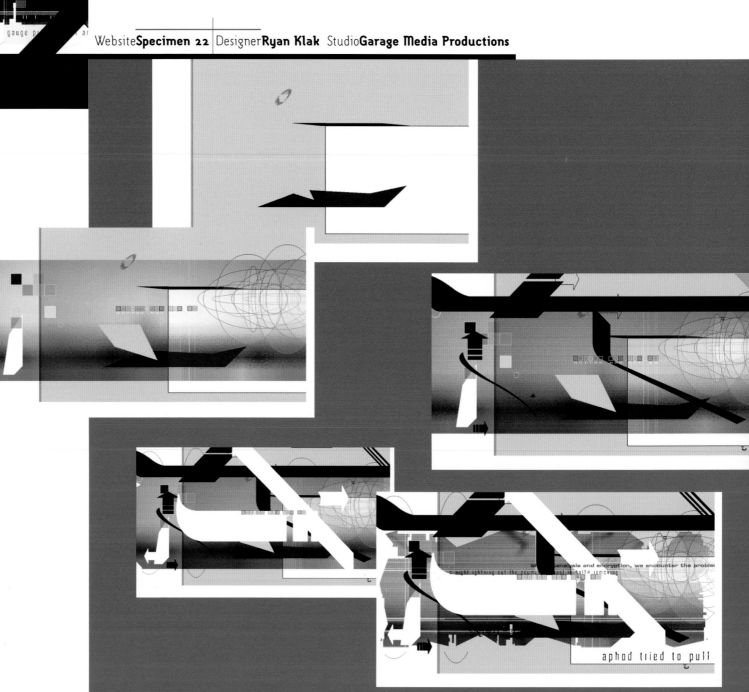

aphod tried to pull

## Specimen 32

Specimen 32, designed by Garage Media's Ryan Klak, reflects a darker mood than others in the Specimen series. This piece is not a parody but rather a composition of intersecting elements. Each proceeding from a very dark environment to a transition where the elements evolve into a complex linear structure. Klak focuses on random design experiments within different browser windows.

**126**

## Specimen 42

Specimen 42, designed by Garage Media's Ryan Klak, reveals another slant of the old "RayGun" design. Not trying to emulate the style, Klak relied on it for inspiration. His intent was to produce randomly something that appear to have taken a lot of time to create. Klak's interests are now heavily focused on random experiments, or shifting designs that change depending on browser window aspects.

**128**

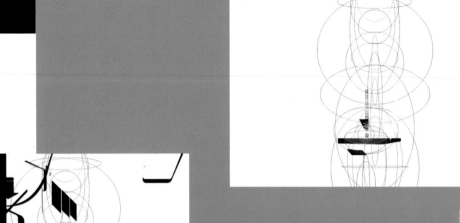

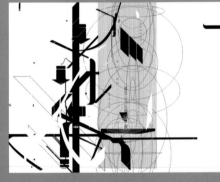

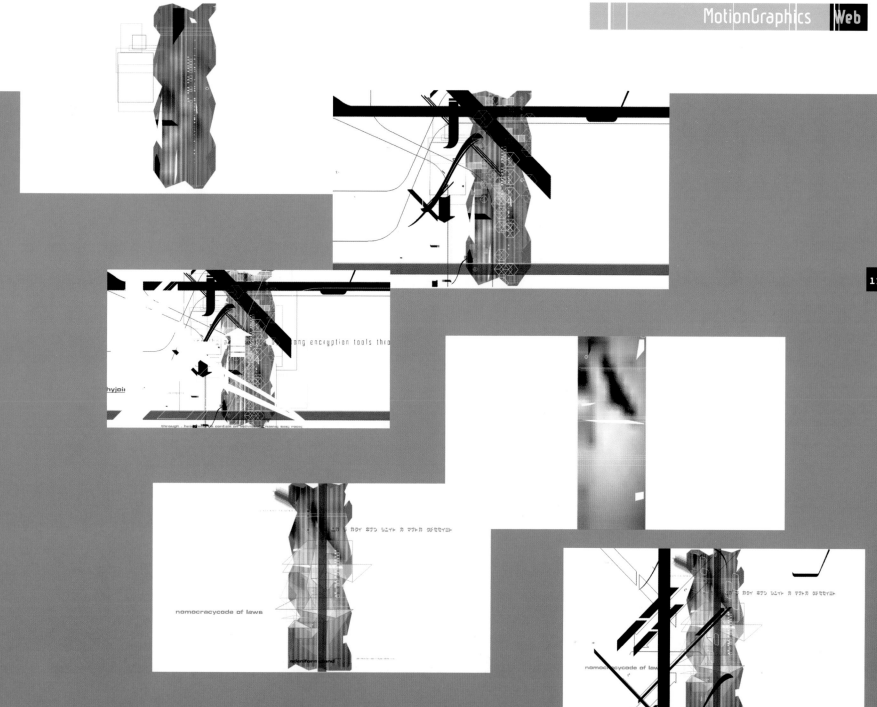

## Specimen 72

Specimen 72, designed by Garage Media's Ryan Klak, combines emerging geometric elements in a monochromatic environment. Klak began the project not based on any particular theme, but as the piece progressed it became more than a parody. The result is, as Klak says, "a combination of 70's string art with a sci-fi temperament." Klak now feels the project has evolved into something much more than the initial premise.

**130**

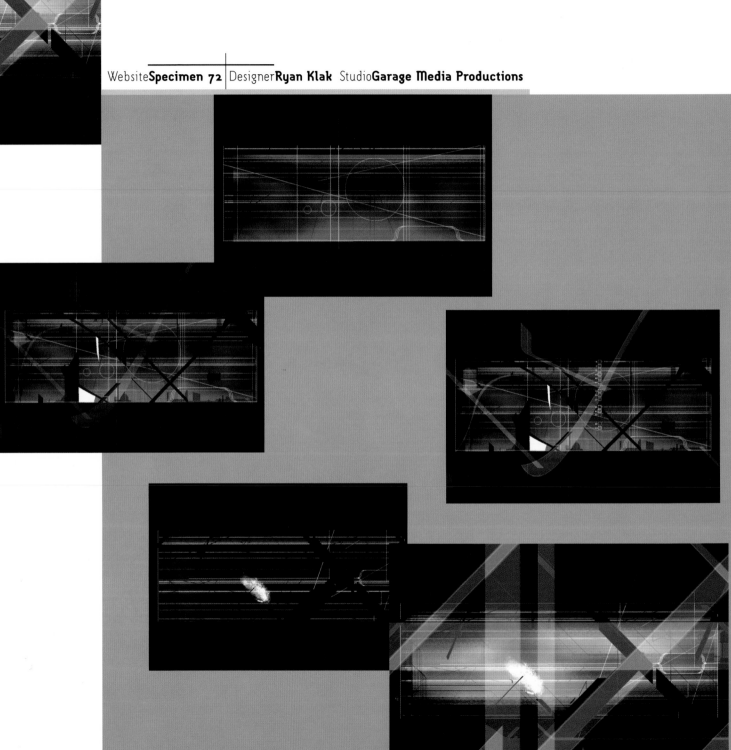

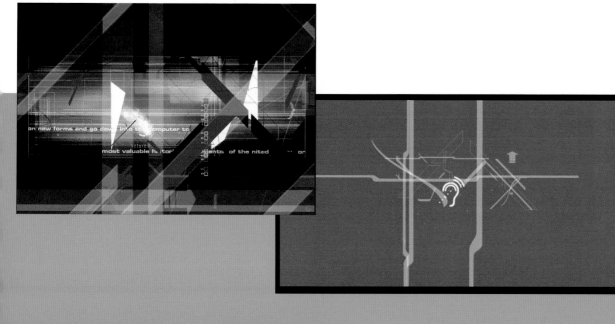

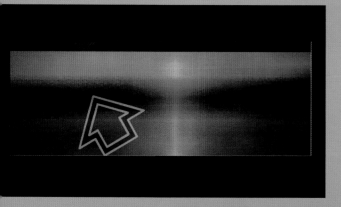

## Specimen 112

Specimen 112, by Garage Media's Ryan Klak, made this version reminiscent of a randomly generated "Wired" designer. Different groups of motion graphic sequences develop with geometric shapes and typographic characters. Some poked fun at magazines or online design, but, according to Klak, "they've outgrown their original intent and become something almost new."

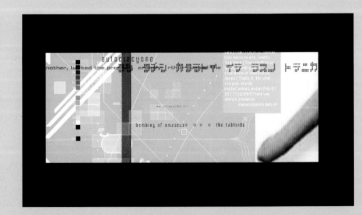

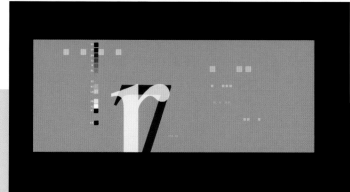

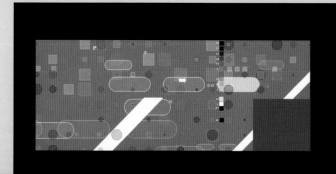

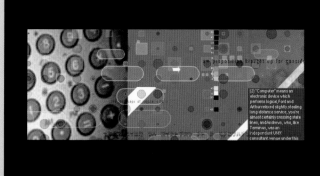

**Specimen 142**

134

Specimen 142 was designed by Garage Media's Ryan Klak as a parody to digital "wallpaper." The motifs are sequenced in a variety of colors. The result is a different design for each based upon a similar one that is anything but original. A member of the resourceful team at Vancouver's Blast Radius, Klak had certain targets in mind when creating each piece for the Specimen project.

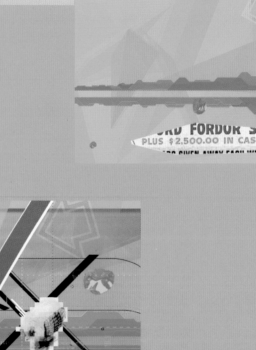

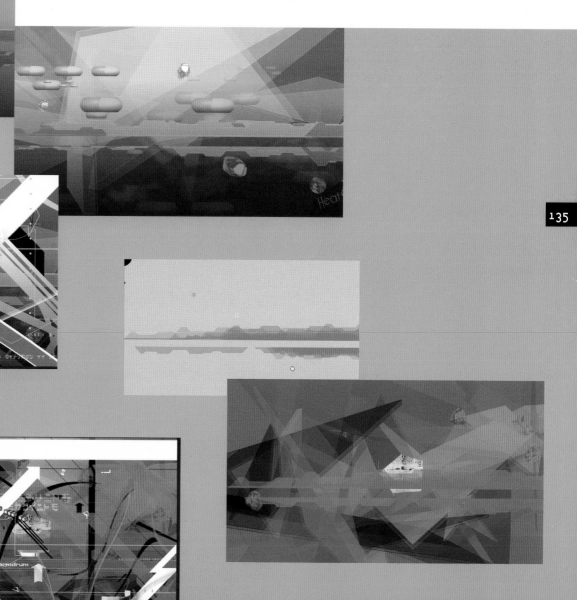

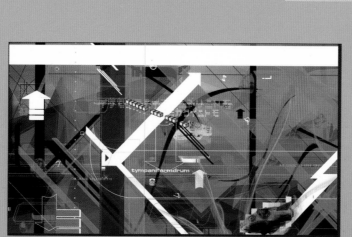

## RockShox Incorporated

San Francisco based twenty2product designed this Y2K site for Rockshox, a manufacturer of bicycle suspension products. The studio also developed a companion video to introduce site navigation conventions at a trade show before the site launch. The site's purpose was to motivate an informed and technically-oriented audience to buy RockShox products, or specify OEM bikes that use the company's product line. Colorful and exciting, with a self-evident navigation system, the RockShox site effectively delivers information while maintaining visual interest. In addition to developing creative solutions for new media, twenty2product's client work appears in title design, broadcast identity and motion graphics for commercials.

Copyright ©2000 RockShox Inc.

**136**

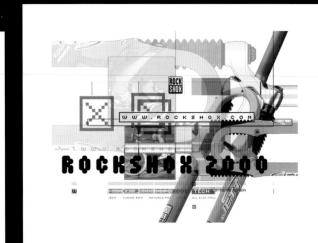

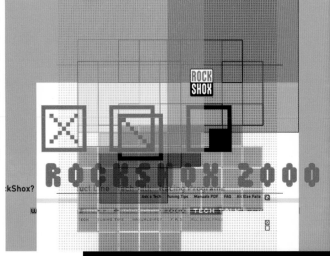

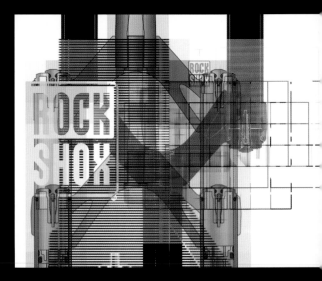

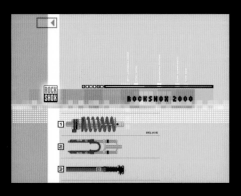

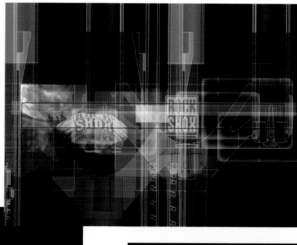

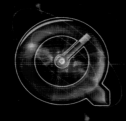

## Apple QuickTime Logo Animations

A favorite project at twenty2product, these QuickTime Logo Animations gave the studio its first experience working with a client that affords them complete freedom. Apple's carte blanche approach made it possible for 22p to exceed the scope of their contracted deliverables. The designers remixed animations in progress, using rough early versions as mattes for incorporating color-correction, filtering, etc., into more expanded animations. Redrawing the logo was necessary to make it symmetrical enough to support transitions from progressive circle outlines. Fortunately, the changes were minimal enough to escape detection by Apple's "logo police."

QuickTime Logo animations Copyright ©2000 Apple Computer, Inc.

138

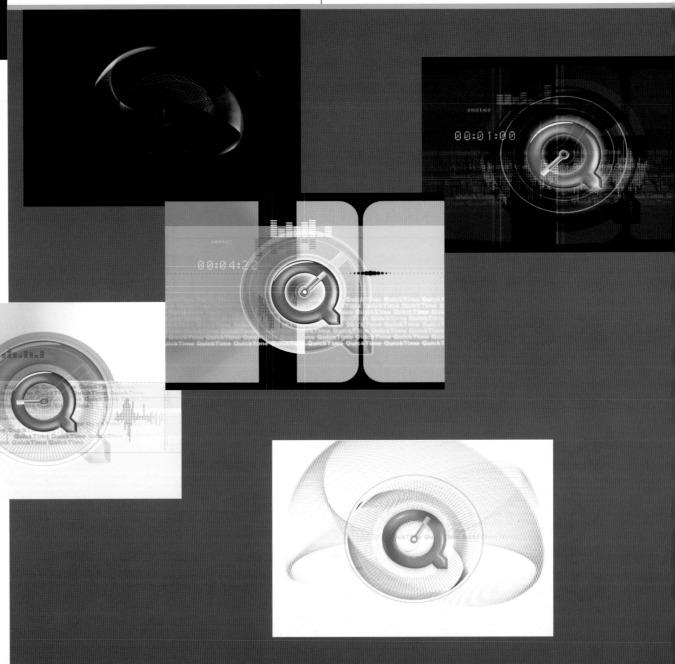

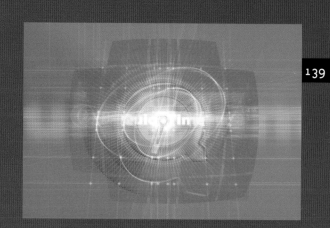

139

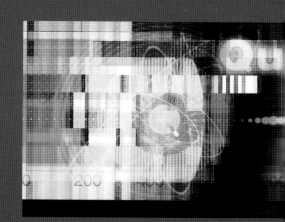

## BP Logo Animations

Twenty2product's logo animations for BP were similar in approach to the QuickTime project, but focused more on spinning off variations for use in secondary applications like **140** websites and plasma screen lobby signage. 22p created 25 versions over the course of three weeks. First, they built a catalog of primitives including blossoming outlines of logo geometry and green-to-white color progressions. Next, Tolson animated these base elements into the initial logo signatures and looping backgrounds. The designers developed additional variations based on light flares "that took too long to render but looked really great."

## EA Sports BIG Logo Animations

Chris Adams, the client from the RockShox project, returned to twenty2product for a series of logo animations for "BIG," EA's new brand of extreme sports video games. Adams structured a catalog of graphic motifs that supported EA's branding, which Terry Green sampled to establish the look and feel for the animations. During Green's sketching process, Nori-zso Tolson worked with the logo, determining the best way to assemble, reveal and deconstruct it. Finally, the design team decided which animations worked best with each layout. This client's audience, noted for its extremely short attention span, required finished animations in the 3 to 1.5 second range.

EA Sports BIG Logo animations Copyright ©2001 Electronic Arts Inc.

142

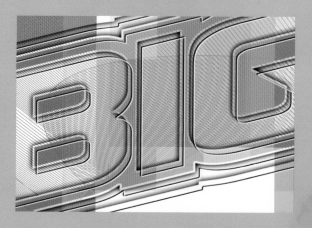

# SEX

**Adams Outdoor**

**144**

Planet Propaganda created this short movie to encapsulate the power of outdoor advertising—billboards. Adams Outdoor's CEO charged the creative shop with the task of developing an attitude-loaded film that he could use to communicate to employees and clients the impact that Adams and outdoor advertising can offer. The piece was presented on the Adams Outdoor website, in laptop presentations and at company gatherings. This unique, multi-purpose project, with its humorous imagery, funky typography and button-pushing text, performed a not so subliminal seduction of its audience.

Studio**Planet Propaganda**

FREE BEER

N A K E D

SEX

0 34100 17215 2

S H O C K

IN LIFE, SOME THINGS

YOUR MESSAGE SHOULD BE ONE OF THEM

THONGS

Out There Thinking.

ADAMS OUTDOOR ADVERTISING

## Artville

146 Planet Propaganda designed this series of quirky Flash pieces to correspond with the colorful Artville print catalogs touting the company's royalty-free stock imagery. Photography and illustration from the Artville library was animated and presented with audio at Artville.com, bringing the brand to life and demonstrating what is possible with the company's diverse collection of images. Planet's short animations continued the Artville tradition of displaying a sense of humor in their effective marketing efforts.

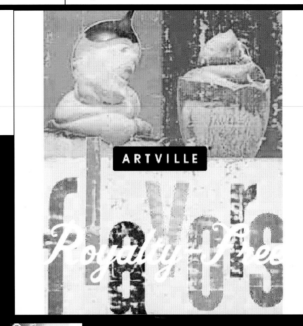

**Brian Wilson** Studio**Planet Propaganda**

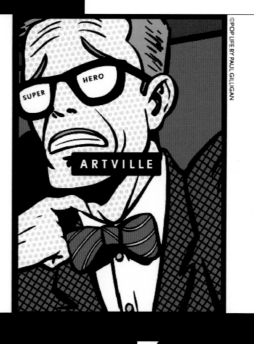

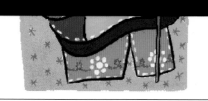

BUILT TO TAKE A BEATING,
GIVE ONE.

Consumer Website**Thormx Website** Designer**Corey Szopinski** Studio**Planet Propaganda**

## Thormx Website

Thor, manufacturers of motocross clothing and gear, challenged Planet Propaganda to develop a website with real attitude. Motocross is all about testosterone-fueled young men racing their machines through mud and air as fast as possible in an attempt to get there first. Colorful and exciting, the site evokes a sense of history—Thor was actually the first company to market in this category. The online promo also publicizes Thor's product line, while introducing the faces behind the brand.

148

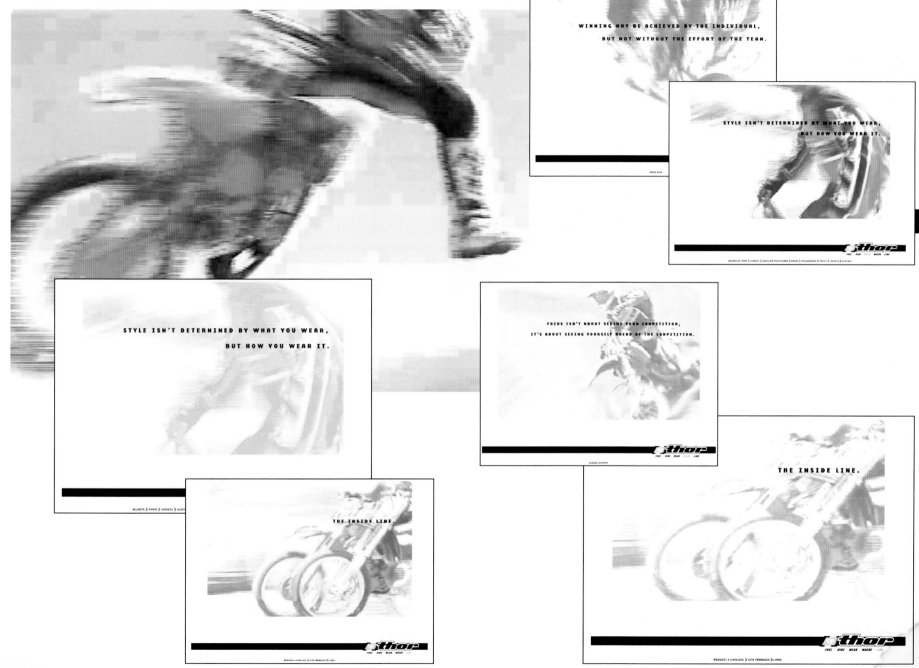

sushi is the best food.

## Jason Zada Demo Reel

Showcasing a varied body of work ranging from interactive media to traditional film and video was a challenge for Evolution Bureau Creative Director Jason Zada. Pulling material from several hundred projects, Zada elected to move through cycles in his demo reel. Beginning with a collage of interactive, film, video and print, the reel quickly splits into various parts, seamlessly displaying each medium in its own section. Zada used Apple's Final Cut Pro as a canvas to experiment, mix, edit and composite all of the pieces together to form the finished presentation, a 2.5 minute mix of work set to a funky musical track.

**150**

sushi is the best food.

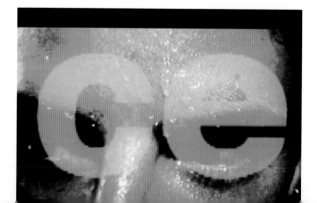

OVERALL THREA

00.006%

OVERALL THREAT = 00.006 %

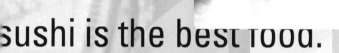

sushi is the best food.

NUTTER

sushi is the best food.

## Sony Style

Electronics giant Sony expounds the concept "simple and smart." The theme was expressed faithfully in this video project from the creative team at Tokyo's Drawing and Manual. The smooth movement of the piece was drawn from a strong foundation of still graphic design, with floating product shots and rotating wireframe imagery emphasizing the sexy lines of headphones and digital cameras. A simple color palette of silver, red, black and white maintains a clean, fresh look. Typography is minimal, with logo motion taking priority during the video. Five separate images synchronize as the "Sony Style" logo emerges, strengthening the brand name throughout a stylish showcase of Sony products.

**152**

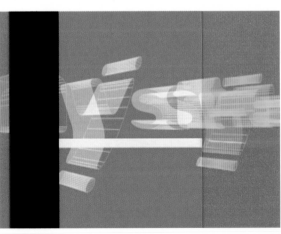

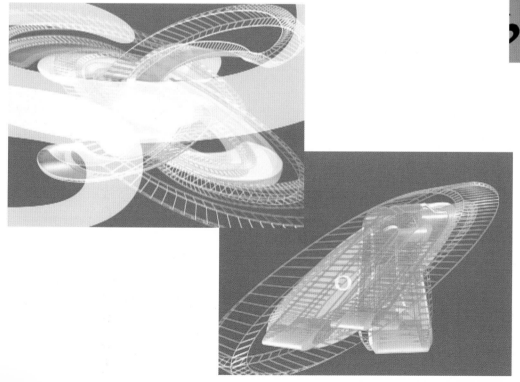

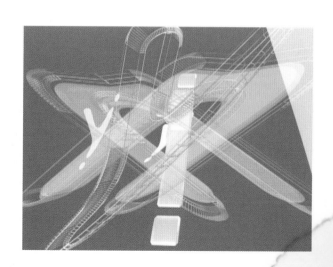

# ARSEREMOS

OPERA is the collaborative design team behind ARSEREMOS, a multimedia project developed for newitalianblood.com, an interactive architecture competition. A group of designers working in virtual space, OPERA is driven by a self-directed consequence of space becoming critical. The work is the propagation of anonymous modular intelligent units building an audience of energy. The creative forces behind OPERA embrace the romance of man and machine, operating in primitive assemblages constructed around the essence of the untimely. The designers are "personal multiple singularities of intensities raking humanity over an intolerably creative edge," says OPERA member Nathan Colkitt. "OPERA is the work in a desolate void, the birth of art at ground zero."

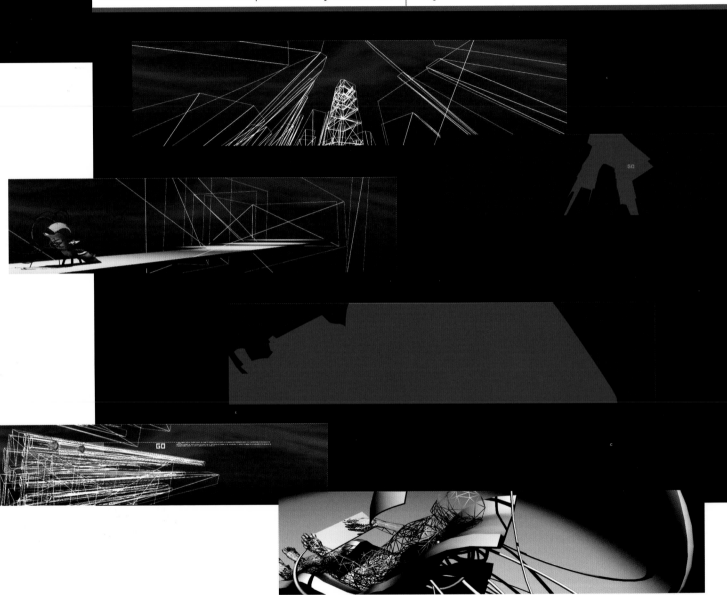

**Gregory Depena, David Schafer** Group Name**OPERA**

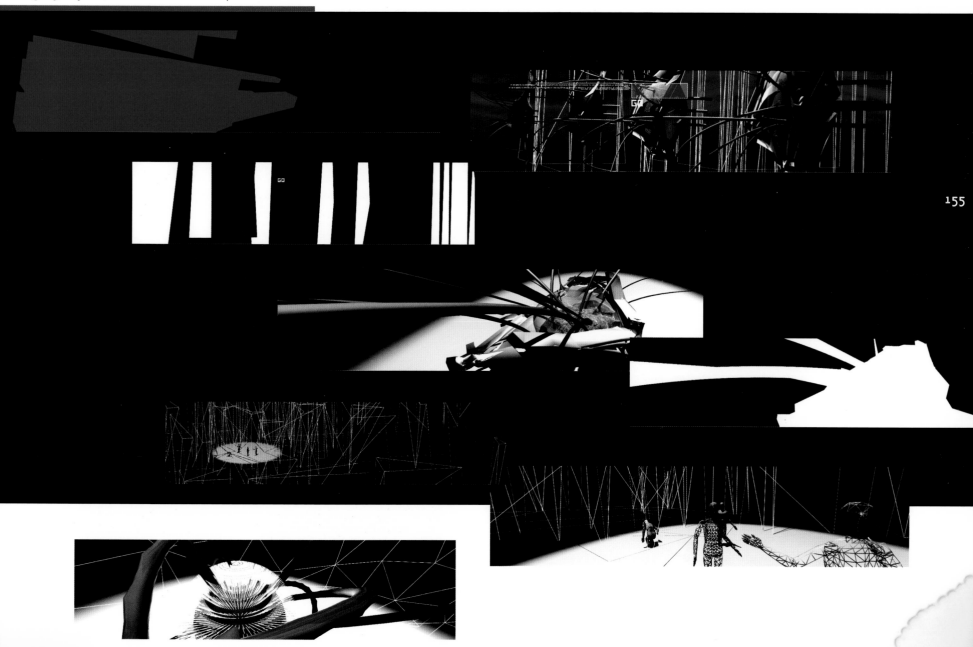

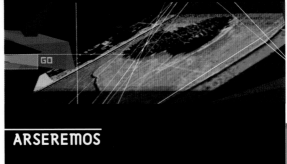

## ARSEREMOS

OPERA brings to life ARSEREMOS, a multimedia project developed for newitalianblood.com, an interactive architecture competition. The collaborative design group, OPERA, invokes the tale of their obscure and opaque vision, "The world is all around and I have gone, vanished. All that is left are my tools, the only part of me that is real. My tools make sense of life's inhumanity and provide a comforting nothingness to my being. My tools are more of me than I could ever be for myself. Space is no longer something I build in, it is space I build with. Brave and bold, I am born unto a new frontier of space, tool and interface. I console the tools and interface fragments of past worlds into oblivion."

156

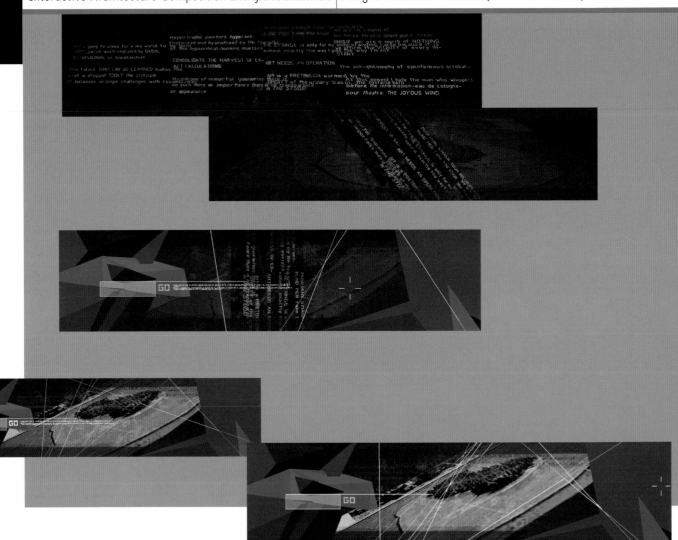

**Gregory Depena, David Schafer** Group Name**OPERA**

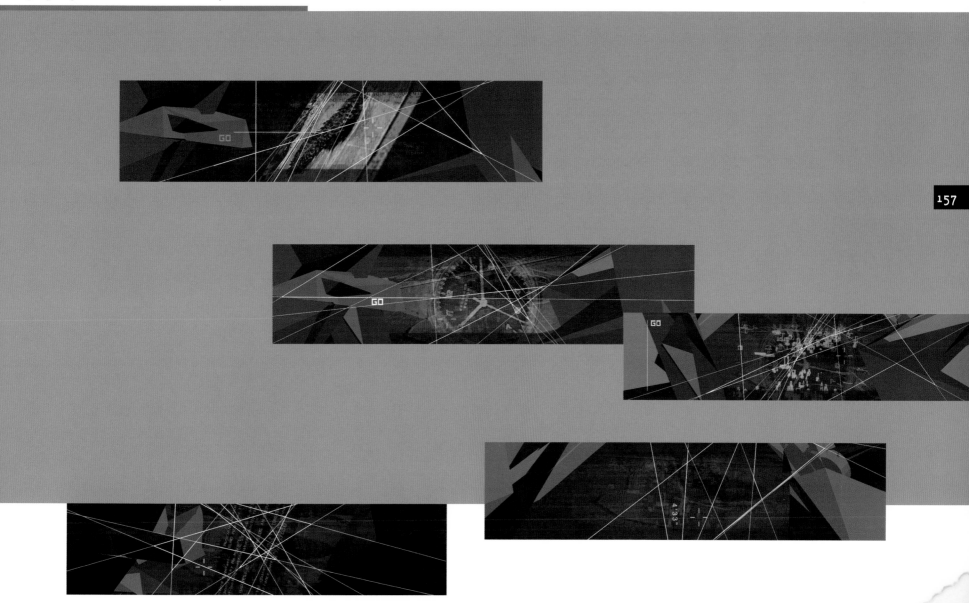

## Directory Index

Juxt Interactive 20–27
Todd Purgason
858 Production Place
Newport Beach, CA 92663
United States
Phone: 949.752.5898
Fax: 949.574.5922
Email: toddhead@juxtinteractive.com
Website: http://www.juxtinteractive.com

Karma Graphix 16–17
Jeremy Grubaugh
1175 Pine Street #1
San Francisco, CA 94105
United States
Phone: 415.673.6734
Fax: 415.276.6361
Email: jeremy@karmagraphix.com
Website: http://www.karmagraphix.com

Lokiss 114–123
Paris, France
Phone: 33(0)6.81.47.32.23
Email: lokiss@lokiss.com
Websites: http://www.lokiss.com
http://www.pornografux.com

Lunchbox Studios 14–15
Adam Roe / Creative Director
43 West 16th Street #7E
New York, NY 10011
United States
Phone: 212.337.8843
Email: info@lunchboxstudios.com
Website: http://www.lunchboxstudios.com

Move Design 58–61
Samuel Lising / Peter Spreenberg
701 Sutter Street / 5th Floor
San Francisco, CA 94109
United States
Phone: 415.202.9880
Fax: 415.202.9881
Email: info@movedesign.com
Website: http://www.movedesign.com

mY pEt sKeLeTOn 52–53
Vincent Marcone
9 Lodge Street #407
Waterloo, Ontario N2J 4S8
Canada

Phone: 519.747.7306
Email: vincent@mypetskeleton.com
Website: http://www.mypetskeleton.com

OPERA 154–157
United States
Websites: Michael Sablone | hypergeneric.com
Nathan Colkitt | nomitage.com
Gregory Depena | polyarch.com
David Schafer | ifitsaperfectday.com

Michal Oppitz 54–55
Freelance Designer
Rencova 36
Brno 621 00 Czech Republic
Phone: +420.5.41226827
Email: monkey@monkey.cz
Websites: http://www.monkey.cz
http://www.isolate.cz

Platinum Design, Inc. 10–13
Estee Pouleris / Vice President
627 Greenwich Street / 11 Floor
New York, NY 10014
United States
Phone: 212.366.4000
Fax: 212.366.4046
Email: epouleris@platinum-design.com
Website: http://www.platinum-design.com

Planet Propaganda 144–149
Kevin Wade
605 Williamson Street
Madison, WI 53703
United States
Phone: 608.256.0000
Fax: 608.256.1975
Email: hank@planetpropaganda.com
Website: http://www.planetpropaganda.com

R/GA 44–47
Robert M. Greenberg / Founder / Chairman / Chief Creative Officer
350 West 39th Street
New York, NY 10018
United States
Phone: 212.946.4000
Fax: 212.946.4010
Email: web@rga.com
Website: http://www.rga.com

scrEAm taBÚ 56–57
Rafael Ferrando Flores
Urb. Cerrogrande, Becerril de la Sierra
Madrid 28940 Spain
Phone: +34.619.87.13.72
Email: rafael@screamtabu.com
Website: http://www.screamtabu.com

Alex Shoukas 34–39
Toronto, Ontario
Canada
Phone: 416.921.2239
Email: alex@massivenumedia.com
Website: http://www.d-realm.net

twenty2product 136–143
San Francisco, CA
United States
Email: info@twenty2.com
Website: http://www.twenty2.com

UZIK 32–33, 40–41
Jean-Marie Tassy
49, Rue de Clery
Paris 75002 France
Phone: 6+33(0)6.62.73.29.86
Email: jm@uzik.com
Website: http://www.uzik.com

Carlo Vega 88–89
319 West 137th Street #1B
New York, NY 10030
United States
Phone: 646.548.0638 / 646.418.3114
Email: digitalpimp@graffodisiak.com
Website: http://www.graffodisiak.com

WDDG 48–51
174 Hudson Street / 3rd Floor
New York, NY 10013
United States
Phone: 646.221.8556
Fax: 413.803.7255
Email: wddg@wddg.com
Website: http://www.wddg.com